An Introduction to the SEC

K. FRED SKOUSEN

Director, Institute of Professional Accountancy
Graduate School of Management
Brigham Young University

SECOND EDITION

Published by

SOUTH-WESTERN PUBLISHING CO.

A29

CINCINNATI   WEST CHICAGO, ILL.   DALLAS   PELHAM MANOR, N.Y.   PALO ALTO, CALIF.

PREFACE

In a free enterprise economy, such as is found in the United States, continued growth and stability require a healthy flow of capital from private and institutional investors to the managements of business enterprises. Capital markets and private financing are the media in the U.S. by which such exchanges occur.

The Securities and Exchange Commission was established in 1934 in an effort to foster honest and open securities markets. Congress, in establishing the SEC, gave broad powers to the Commission to regulate securities and to ensure proper financial reporting and disclosure by American businesses.

The importance of the SEC and its dealings with the business community in general and the accounting profession in particular is, in the view of the author, unquestionable. Accounting and financial periodicals frequently carry announcements of some new accounting rule or the liability of an accountant or business executive under the Securities Acts. Many accounting, legal, and consulting firms derive a major part of their revenues from activities directly or indirectly related to the SEC. For accountants, these activities range from the certification of financial statements used in registrations under the various Securities Acts to the giving of advice on the applicability of different provisions of the Acts.

The purpose of this book, in a narrow sense, is to acquaint the reader with the nature, origin, and workings of the SEC, particularly as related to the accounting profession. In a broader sense, this book deals with the informational needs and requirements relative to the capital markets. Hopefully, the reader will be able to see the relationship between investment decisions (by both investors and managers), capital markets regulation by the SEC, and the role of the accountant and business executive relative to both.

The book is structured to accomplish these purposes. The first chapter gives a historical background to securities legislation in the U.S. and explains the structure and work of the SEC. Chapter 2 examines the legal framework of the SEC, with a brief explanation of each major Act administered by the Commission. Also included is a description of the accountant's primary duties under each Act. Chapter 3 focuses attention on the registration process and the reporting requirements, primarily under the 1933 and 1934 Acts. An approach to researching SEC accounting-related problems is also discussed. A comparative analysis between reports presented to shareholders and those submitted to the SEC is given in Chapter 4. Actual examples are presented to highlight the comparisons. The final chapter looks at the extensive interaction between the SEC and the business community, including liability under the Securities Acts, disclosure requirements, regulation of the accounting profession, and the ongoing critical issue of determining generally accepted accounting principles. An appendix containing an annotated bibliography gives further guidance into SEC research and provides valuable information for those wishing to augment the material presented in this book.

In view of the impact of the SEC on business and the accounting profession, it is unfortunate that so little attention is given to the subject in the typical business and accounting curriculum. Some lengthy technical books on the subjects covered in this text are used by professionals. The bibliography provides selected references. This introductory text attempts to summarize detail and to synthesize technicalities in a readable, useful manner for accounting and business students. The more detailed books are not entirely suited for classroom instruction. Hopefully, this book will fill a perceived need for an introduction to the SEC.

Although intended primarily as a supplement to intermediate accounting, auditing, and accounting theory classes, the book can easily be used in other classes to provide an overview of the SEC and its importance to business in general. This is especially needed in graduate accounting or MBA programs where such exposure has not been provided previously. The book should establish a basis for further study and research on the separate topics described herein.

This book is the result of the efforts of many people. Personal gratitude and the principle of full and fair disclosure require that I acknowledge these contributions collectively, if not individually. Special recognition and thanks are given to Mei-Ling Yang and Stan Duffin, who provided significant assistance in preparing the second edition. J. Kent Millington assisted significantly in the research and preparation of the original edition. Appreciation is also expressed to David R. Anderson and Michael D. Olsen of Valtek Incorporated for their cooperation and assistance in providing many of the exhibits contained herein; to RaNae Allen for typing and proofing drafts of the manuscript; and to numerous students and colleagues and my family for their encouragement and assistance while writing and revising this book. Notwithstanding the involvement of others, the responsibility for any deficiencies in this book must be assumed solely by the author.

K. Fred Skousen

CONTENTS

CHAPTER 2   LEGAL FRAMEWORK OF THE SEC 18

CHAPTER I

ORIGIN AND NATURE
OF THE SEC

The Securities and Exchange Commission (SEC) was established in 1934 to help regulate the United States securities market. Since that time, the SEC has played a very important role in the business community. This chapter deals with the reasons for the establishment of the SEC, its organizational structure, and the nature of its current operations. To provide a proper perspective, the corporate form of business, capital markets, and the need for disclosure of financial information are discussed.

Historical Background

In the early days of commerce, the economic system was basically a barter economy. Goods and services were traded directly for other goods and services. Businesses were conducted as proprietorships or perhaps as partnerships and joint ventures. Generally, the management and the owners were the same individuals. External reporting of the results of operations by these closely held commercial entities was simply not needed. Internal information for planning and control was needed, however, and accounting systems were introduced to help provide that information.

Establishment and Early Regulation of Capital Markets

As commercial enterprises multiplied, both in size and number, more and more people were attracted to business opportunities, and the investment of capital resources expanded rapidly. The more aggressive businesses soon realized the lucrative advantage of encouraging capital investment by people who were willing to assume the risks of ownership but in most cases were neither willing nor able to assist in management. An advantage of the developing corporate form of business was that ownership and financial interest could be spread over a broad base by the issuing of securities. Ownership and management thus became separated, and there was a need for a marketplace where equity and debt securities could be exchanged for invested capital resources. This need led to the establishment of extensive capital markets, first in Europe and then in the United States.

The corporate form of business also increased the need for objective verification of data and created a need for disclosure in the form of more and better information to owners and potential investors. As capital markets increased in size and activity, an irresponsible attitude developed in some corporate officers who took advantage of lax conditions in the securities markets and profited by distortions and manipulations. Governments, sensing some responsibility to protect those who invested in corporations, made faltering attempts to create a working partnership between management and investors and to ensure an adequate supply of capital available for sound economic growth.

For example, in 1285, King Edward I attempted to gain some control over burgeoning capital markets by authorizing the Court of Aldermen to license brokers located in London. In the early 18th century, France and England experienced a mania of speculative investment centered around the development of trading companies doing business in the Western Hemisphere. At one point, scheme offers exceeded £ 300,000,000 in the aggregate—more than the value of all the land in Great Britain.[1] Parliament was incensed over the abuses and retaliated with the harsh Bubble Act of 1720, holding issuers and brokers liable for damages and losses resulting from dishonest issues of securities.

Regulation of Securities in the U.S.

The pattern of securities legislation in the United States followed the example of Great Britain: widespread abuses, made obvious by a financial crisis, were followed by a series of retrospective investigations leading to the passage of restrictive laws imposed on securities markets.

A popular misconception is that securities regulation in the United States stems only from the crash of the stock market in 1929 and the ensuing years of financial stagnation. The financial difficulties of the 1930s only provided the last straw, the impetus, to pass securities legislation in the United States.

---

[1] Louis Loss, *Securities Regulation* (Boston: Little, Brown, & Co., 1961), p. 4.

Early Federal Attempts. Federal securities legislation had been sought since the late 19th century. In 1885, discussion concerned federal licensing of companies involved in interstate commerce. The Federal Trade Commission Act and the Clayton Act resulted from efforts at federal control during the first years of this century. The Industrial Commission, established by Congress in 1898, reported in 1902 that public disclosure of material information of all publicly held corporations should be mandatory and should include annual financial reports. During the next two decades, three major bills seeking greater disclosure were introduced into Congress but none were ever reported out of committee to either the House or the Senate. The time was not right; a serious financial plight was not in recent memory to spur such legislation.

State Regulation. While the federal government was searching for its role in securities legislation, state governments were making some attempts to bring order to chaotic securities markets. Kansas led the way in 1911 to combat the bleeding of the "Agrarian West" by the "Moneyed East."[2] By 1913, 22 other states had passed laws aimed at regulating the sale of securities. Divided into two categories, these laws were: (1) fraud laws, which imposed penalties if evidence indicated fraud had been committed in the sale of securities; and (2) regulatory laws, which attempted to prohibit the sale of securities until an application was filed and permission was granted by the state.[3] These early laws became known as "blue-sky" laws after a judicial decision characterized some transactions as "speculative schemes that have no more basis than so many feet of blue sky."[4]

State laws, for several reasons, never proved really effective in regulating securities markets. Of primary consideration was the interstate nature of the U.S. economic system. The absence of legislation in some states and the inadequacy of laws in others allowed fraudulent and deceptive practices to continue in spite of regulatory efforts. A study submitted by the Department of Commerce in 1933 indicated that "the most effective and widely used method of evading the provision of state blue-sky laws consists of operating across state lines."[5]

Another reason for the inadequacy of state laws was the seeming

---

[2] *Ibid.*, p. 18.

[3] V. Geiger-Jones, 242 U.S. 339, quoted in J.K. Lasser and J.A. Gerardi, *Federal Securities Act Procedures* (New York: McGraw-Hill Book Co., 1934), p. 2.

[4] *Ibid.*

[5] U.S. Department of Commerce, *A Study of the Economic and Legal Aspects of the Proposed Federal Securities Act,* Hearings before House Committee on Interstate and Foreign Commerce on H.R. 4314, 73d Congress, 1st Session, 1933, p. 87.

reluctance on the part of state legislatures to provide proper enforcement of the laws they had established. State legislatures seemed more
concerned about having a law on the books than about enforcing proper
regulation of securities sales.

Exemptions contained in the blue-sky laws were additional in-
adequacies of state legislation. Complicating state enforcement was the
nearly universal willingness of victims to condone the offense or to
accept a compromise. If a state began preparing evidence against a corporation, the company would pay investors for a part of the loss, caus-
ing the state to lose its witnesses and the case.

Abuses of the 1920s. The securities market activities of the 1920s are
legend. While trading and investment were brisk, the underlying
strength of the market was eroding as a result of certain common practices.[6] The first was price manipulation. It was not uncommon for
broker or dealers to indulge in "wash sales" or "matched orders" where
successive buy and sell orders created a false impression of activity and
forced prices up. This maneuver allowed those involved to reap huge
profits before the price fell back to its true market level. Outright deceit
by issuing false and misleading statements was another improper practice. These manipulative procedures had as their objective the making of
profits at the expense of unwary investors.

Another practice undermining securities markets was the excessive
use of credit to finance speculative activities. This is commonly referred
to as buying stocks "on margin." There was no limit to the amount of
credit a broker could extend to a customer. As a result, a slight decline in
market prices could start a chain reaction which would gain momentum
when an overextended customer sold out because a margin could not be
covered. Such a situation became critical when the market began to
decline drastically late in 1929 and early in 1930.

The misuse of corporate information by corporate officials and other
"insiders" was still another practice that led to instability in the securities markets. While positioning themselves to take advantage of fluctua-
tions in stock prices when the news became public, executive officers
often withheld information about corporate activities.

Edward R. Willet has described the overall situation:

> The public outcry arising from the great decline in stock prices between
> 1929 and 1933 motivated the passage of the major federal laws regulat-

---

[6] Securities and Exchange Commission, *25th Annual Report*, 1959, pp. XV-XVIL. The
Foreword to this report is obviously an attempt to support the SEC, but it does provide
valuable information about the background of the SEC.

ing the securities industry. During the late 1920s investors speculated excessively. About 55 percent of all personal savings were used to purchase securities and the public was severely affected when the Dow Jones Industrial Average fell 89 percent between 1929 and 1933.

During this period, security price manipulation was common and satisfactory information concerning securities usually was not available. Regulation was badly needed. It is fortunate that legislation passed during such a period of strong reaction against the industry seems to have been basically good legislation.[7]

Awakening to the Need. As state laws proved ineffective, government officials became concerned that "a supplemental federal law was needed to stop this gap through which were being wasted hundreds of millions of public savings that might otherwise have been diverted to substantial industrial development."[8] The aggregate value of all stocks listed on the New York Stock Exchange was $89 billion before the market declined in the fall of 1929. In September and October, the aggregate value dropped by $18 billion. After those two disastrous months, it appeared for a short time that a recovery was under way, but the market softened in the spring of 1930, and a bear market prevailed over the next two and one-half years. In 1932, the aggregate value of stocks was only $15 billion—a drop of $74 billion from 1929.

The transition from state to federal regulation was not without contest, however, or without a traumatic awakening to the need for federal legislation. As Loss points out, "Whether any legislation could prevent another such catastrophe is beside the point; it is a simple fact that the developments of 1929-1932 brought the long movement for federal securities regulation to a head."[9]

Federal Action. In March, 1932, the Senate passed a resolution allowing the Banking and Currency Committee to investigate the securities industry. The subsequent far-reaching investigation uncovered a variety of evils. A report to the House of Representatives highlighted the extent of losses incurred by the investing public due to the practices of issuers and brokers:

During the postwar decade some 50 billions of new securities were floated in the United States. Fully half or $25,000,000,000 worth of securities floated during this period have been proved to be worthless.

---

[7] Edward R. Willet, *Fundamentals of Securities Markets* (New York: Appleton-Century-Crofts, 1968), p. 211.

[8] Lasser and Gerardi, *op. cit.*, p. 4.

[9] Loss, *op. cit.*, p. 75.

These cold figures spell tragedy in the lives of thousands of individuals who invested their life savings, accumulated after years of effort, in these worthless securities. The flotation of such a mass of essentially fraudulent securities was made possible because of the complete abandonment by many underwriters and dealers in securities of those standards of fair, honest, and prudent dealing that should be basic to the encouragement of investment in any enterprise.

Alluring promises of easy wealth were freely made with little or no attempt to bring to the investor's attention those facts essential to estimating the worth of any security. High pressure salesmanship rather than careful counsel was the rule in this most dangerous of enterprises.

Equally significant with these countless individual tragedies is the wastage that this irresponsible selling of securities has caused to industry.[10]

Several philosophies prevailed as Congress approached the task of legislation. Many advocated a fraud law patterned after New York's Martin Act. These protagonists saw preventive laws as unworkable, unenforceable hindrances to honest business. Those at the other extreme wanted laws patterned after the laws of several other states that required securities registration and strict qualification. A compromise group spoke for disclosure laws similar to the English Companies Act of 1900.[11]

Establishment of the SEC

With disclosure being the main concern, Congress sought securities regulation that would blend the various philosophies. The results were the Securities Act of 1933 and the Securities Exchange Act of 1934. It was under the authority of the latter act that the Securities and Exchange Commission was created. The SEC was given the duty to ensure "full and fair" disclosure of all material facts concerning securities offered for public investment. The Commission's intent was not necessarily to prevent speculative securities from entering the market, but to insist that investors be provided with adequate information. Initiation of litigation in cases of fraud and provision for the proper registration of securities are two supplemental objectives of the SEC.

---

[10] *Federal Supervision of Traffic in Investment Securities in Interstate Commerce*, H.R. Report No. 85, 73d Congress, 1st Session, 1933.
[11] Loss, *op. cit.*, pp. 76-77.

Reflections on the Establishment of the SEC. The view that the SEC was established to cure improper and unethical business practices with respect to capital markets is not held by some individuals, especially some academic researchers. For example, George Benston has concluded from his research that there is little justification for the accounting disclosure requirements of the 1933 and 1934 Acts.[12] Benston found little evidence of fraud in connection with financial statements during the period prior to the enactment of the Securities Acts. His research further suggests that the data required by the SEC do not seem to be particularly useful to investors. Thus, while Benston does see an impact on the accounting profession by the SEC, he does not see the impact of the SEC being of direct or positive benefit to the securities markets.

Benston's viewpoint runs counter to the underlying justification of the SEC. In a 1975 interview, John C. Burton, then Chief Accountant for the SEC, stated:

> In a broad sense we hope [disclosure regulations] will contribute to a more efficient capital market . . . . The way in which we hope that will be achieved is first by giving investors more confidence that they are getting the whole story and second by encouraging the development of better tools of analysis and more responsibility on the part of the professional analyst to understand what's going on. We think that by giving them better data we can encourage them in the direction of doing a better job, thus leading, we hope, to more effective capital markets.[13]

Burton's statement implies that the SEC's primary role is to provide information which can be used to make better decisions, which in turn leads to more efficient capital markets. SEC regulation is, therefore, assumed to be in the public interest and holds a close relationship to the informational objective of accounting.[14] A more cynical observation, supported by some research in economics and finance, is that all types of regulation are rooted in self-interest, i.e., business people and politicians create laws to restrict competition and transfer wealth to themselves.[15] Instead of a public-interest assumption, some would argue that the SEC and the accounting profession are founded on a self-

---

[12] George J. Benston, "The Value of the SEC's Accounting Disclosure Requirements," *The Accounting Review* (July, 1969), pp. 515-532.

[13] "An Interview with John C. Burton," *Management Accounting* (May, 1975), p. 21.

[14] For an expanded discussion of the public interest assumption of the SEC and its impact on the informational objective of accounting, see Ross L. Watts and Jerold L. Zimmerman, "The Demand for and Supply of Accounting Theories: The Market for Excuses," *The Accounting Review* (April, 1979), pp. 273-305.

[15] *Ibid.*

interest assumption. In effect, this position was taken by the staff of the U.S. Senate subcommittee which studied the accounting establishment.[16] Their findings and recommendations are considered more fully in Chapter 5.

While recognizing the different points of view concerning why the SEC was established, the author believes that the SEC's primary role is to help regulate the capital markets. The author accepts as valid the public interest justification and the full disclosure objective of the SEC.

Growth of the SEC. The SEC has experienced an interesting life cycle. The infancy and puberty of the Commission extended to 1945 and were characterized by the working out of kinks in legislation and the establishment of the administrative procedures necessary for the new agency. Early commissioners had to be salespeople as much as interpretative geniuses; they inspired confidence in the laws and at the same time enforced them. By 1945 the SEC began to reach maturity. Then, for approximately the next 15 years, the Commission concentrated on performing the function assigned by the laws as interpreted in previous years. This period was characterized by very little significant legislation or innovation. Somewhat wider dissemination of information and greater disclosure resulted during this period, but only by extension of previous laws. In general, the post-World War II years were marked by public confidence in the securities industry.

A new round of legislative inquiry into the adequacy of existing securities legislation was initiated after a market break in May of 1962, which stopped three years of speculative frenzy in glamour stocks. A revitalization of the SEC began, culminating in significant legislation in the 1964 Amendments to the Exchange Act. The 1960s also witnessed a growth of litigation related to the liabilities for the accuracy of registration statements, the provisions for which are contained in Section II of the 1933 Act. In 1970 several years of investigation of investment companies resulted in amendments to the Investment Company Act of 1940. In 1977, the Foreign Corrupt Practices Act was enacted to combat corporate bribery and illegal business practices.

The future of securities markets in general will be influenced greatly by the SEC. Investigations of the 1960s and 1970s have led to some dissatisfaction over the structure of the markets, and the 1980s will likely bring efforts to centralize those security markets having component

---

[16] U.S. Senate Committee on Government Operations, Subcommittee on Reports, Accounting, and Management, *The Accounting Establishment* (Washington: U.S. Government Printing Office, 1977).

parts. Other important probable considerations in the next decade include negotiated commission rates, the influence of large institutional investors, the role of brokers and dealers, the monopoly of the New York Stock Exchange, and the role of smaller exchanges.[17] Whatever the outcome of these issues, the Commission will, no doubt, be an influential partner in corporate financing procedures in future years.

Organizational Structure of the SEC

With this historical background in mind, a closer look at the SEC can now be taken. The SEC is directed by five commissioners, no more than three of whom may be from the same political party. Members of the Commission are appointed by the President of the United States with the approval of the Senate. Each commissioner is appointed for a five-year term with one member's term expiring on June 5 of each year. The President designates one member to chair the Commission.

The SEC is administered from its Washington, D.C. headquarters and has regional and branch offices in the major financial centers of the U.S. The organizational structure is illustrated by Exhibit 1-1 on page 10; the regions of the SEC are shown in Exhibit 1-2 on page 11. The Commission is assisted by a staff of professionals including accountants, engineers, examiners, lawyers, and securities analysts. These professionals are assigned to the various divisions and offices, including the regional offices, shown in the organization chart.

SEC Divisions

A brief look at the duties of the five divisions and several of the principal offices is appropriate at this point.

Division of Corporation Finance. The Division of Corporation Finance is perhaps the most important division for individuals in business and specifically for accountants. The division's major responsibilities include: assisting the Commission in establishing and requiring adherence to standards of economic and financial reporting and disclosure by all companies under SEC jurisdiction; setting standards for the disclosure requirements of proxy solicitations; and administering disclosure requirements for the Securities Act, the Securities Exchange Act, the

---

[17] Harold S. Bloomenthal, *Securities and Federal Corporate Law* (New York: Clark Boardman Co., 1972), pp. 1-7 to 1-13. This reference is an excellent survey of the life cycle of the SEC.

EXHIBIT 1-1

SECURITIES AND EXCHANGE COMMISSION

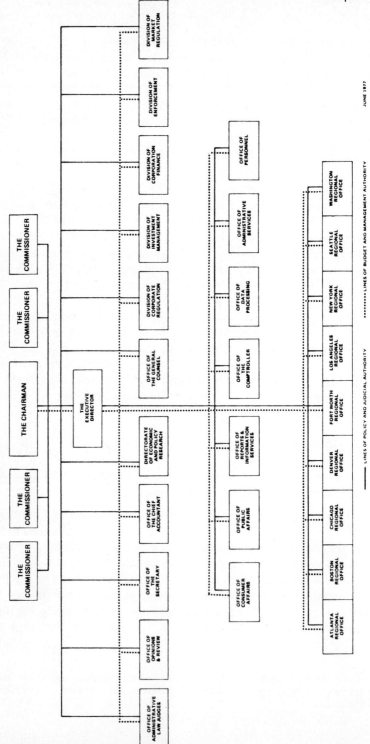

Source: Securities and Exchange Commission, *The Work of the Securities and Exchange Commission* (Washington: U.S. Government Printing Office, 1978).

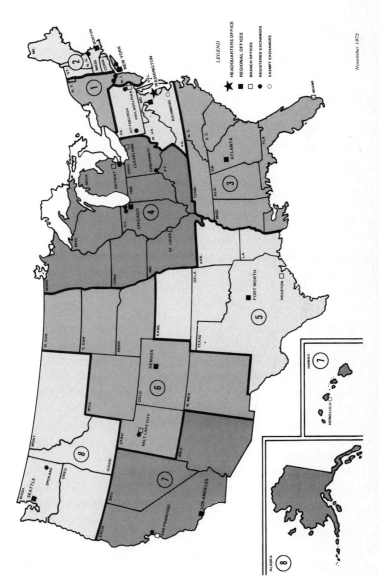

EXHIBIT 1-2

REGIONS OF THE SECURITIES AND EXCHANGE COMMISSION

Source: Securities and Exchange Commission, *The Work of the Securities and Exchange Commission* (Washington: U.S. Government Printing Office, 1978).

Public Utility Holding Company Act, and the Investment Company Act.

The Division of Corporation Finance reviews all registration statements (lengthy and often complicated narrations of corporate operations), prospectuses, quarterly and annual reports, proxy statements, and sales literature. As these reporting devices are explained later in the book, the reader will better understand the significant influence of this division. Investigations, examinations, formal hearings, and informal conferences are used in the analysis and review of the myriad of reports handled each year by this division.

In addition to its review function, the Division of Corporation Finance also provides a useful interpretative and advisory service to help clarify to issuers, accountants, lawyers, and underwriters the application and requirements of the securities laws it administers. Inasmuch as substantially all of the financial statements submitted for review must be certified by independent accountants, a significant portion of an accountant's work with the SEC will be reviewed by this division. The advisory service has proved effective in avoiding problems by providing instructive guidance concerning registration and reporting procedures.

The SEC established the Office of Small Business Policy within the Division of Corporation Finance to assist in the development of rules and regulations designed to aid capital formation for small businesses. This office also processes Form S-18, which is a simplified registration statement for small businesses.

Division of Market Regulation. The Division of Market Regulation assists the Commission in the regulation of national securities exchanges and of brokers and dealers registered under the Investment Advisers Act. This division cooperates with the regional offices in investigating and inspecting exchanges, brokers, and dealers. An active and ongoing surveillance of trading markets, both exchanges and over-the-counter markets, is the means by which the Division of Market Regulation exerts its influence and discharges its responsibilities. The objective of the surveillance is twofold. First, the division attempts to discourage manipulation or fraud in connection with the sale or purchase of securities. Second, the division supervises the issuance of new securities and ensures adherence to rules regarding the stabilization of securities prices. Because the Commission has the power to suspend an exchange for up to one year, the activities of this division are important and powerful.

The Division of Market Regulation also supervises the broker-dealer inspection program. Brokers and dealers are required to register with the SEC and to submit to periodic inspections of their activities. The periodic reports submitted by brokers/dealers are analyzed by this division to ensure proper disclosure and to foster the proper conduct of these dealers. Capable of exerting considerable control over the activities of brokers and dealers, the Commission can, and does, permanently prohibit brokers/dealers from transacting business or, as is usually the case, suspend them for a shorter period of time. Not only does it supervise, it also provides interpretative advice to investors and registrants on the requirements of the statutes it administers. The counselor role has proved effective in avoiding possible problems, thus making the remainder of this division's work easier.

Division of Enforcement. The Division of Enforcement is responsible for the review and direction of all enforcement activities of the regional offices, supervision of investigations conducted pursuant to federal securities laws, and institution of injunctive actions. The Division must determine whether available evidence supports allegations in complaints. Since it is responsible for reviewing cases sent to the Department of Justice for criminal prosecution, this division maintains close cooperation with the Office of the General Counsel.

Division of Corporate Regulation. The Division of Corporate Regulation has two major responsibilities. The first is to help administer the Public Utility Holding Company Act of 1935; the second is to perform the Commission's advisory functions to U.S. district courts under Chapter XI of the Bankruptcy Act for corporations having numerous private stockholders.

The essence of the Public Utility Holding Company Act of 1935 is the requirement that large utilities be physically integrated and regulated to prevent unnecessary complexities in corporate structure. The principal regulatory provision of the Public Utility Holding Company Act gives the SEC power to regulate securities issuances, sales and purchases of securities by utilities, and the interest of utilities in other businesses. Accounting functions and business transactions with affiliates are also regulated by the SEC. To illustrate the extensive work done by the Commission under the Public Utility Holding Company Act of 1935, more securities releases—official pronouncements of policy and procedures—have been given pursuant to the 1935 Act than under any other federal securities law. The Division of Corporate Regulation is responsible for this effort.

Chapter XI of the Bankruptcy Act allows the SEC to act as a disinterested adviser to federal courts in proceedings involving the reorganization of companies with financial difficulties. In conjunction with regional offices, the Division of Corporate Regulation assists the SEC in determining the extent of participation in some proceedings and deciding the Commission's position in a reorganization. Actual court appearances are usually made by General Counsel, but this division must prepare reports and position papers in support of Counsel.

Division of Investment Management Regulation. The Division of Investment Management Regulation assists the SEC in the administration of the Investment Company Act of 1940 and the Investment Advisers Act of 1940. All investigations and inspections arising from these Acts and matters concerning the services provided by investment companies and dealers are responsibilities of this division. Reporting and enforcement requirements are the responsibilities of other divisions, however.

The reader will probably already have noted that some divisions have overlapping authority. Cooperation among divisions is essential if the SEC is to function smoothly. The accounting practitioner and the business executive must be aware of the duplications in order to successfully comply with securities statutes. Compliance with one division's requirements does not automatically ensure adherence to another division's statutes.

Major Offices

For the purposes of this book, an introduction to the principal offices functioning under the Commission is necessary. The numerous regional offices serve as field representatives for the administration and enforcement of federal securities legislation. These offices serve as the eyes and ears of the Commission and have considerable power to initiate investigations into possible violations of securities laws, while working in connection with the five divisions. The *Federal Securities Law Reporter* lists ten functions of regional offices, and seven have to do with investigating powers and authority. The other three functions are related to advisory roles under different Acts.[18]

A major part of the investigative activities conducted by regional offices is concerned with brokers and dealers. All registered dealers are subject to surprise inspections to ensure compliance with statutory provisions related especially to accounting procedures. Accountants serving a broker or dealer should be fully aware of accounting policies related to their client's business.

---

[18] *Federal Securities Law Reporter* (New York: Commerce Clearing House). Pages 1042 to 1052 of Vol. 1 give an excellent description of the organizations of the SEC, listing all divisions and offices. Andrew Downey Orrick has given a thorough study of divisional responsibilities in "Organization, Procedures and Practices of the Securities and Exchange Commission," *George Washington Law Review*, Vol. 28. No. 1 (October, 1959). The organization has changed somewhat since Orrick's article, but it still serves as an excellent source.

Office of the Chief Accountant. The Office of the Chief Accountant provides the Commission with expert advice in matters of accounting and auditing. The goal of the Chief Accountant is the upgrading of accounting and auditing standards that will provide the disclosure the Commission seeks. The SEC has been given statutory power to develop accounting principles. The Chief Accountant, who is primarily responsible, directs the development of administrative policy concerning accounting matters and the preparation of accounting rules and regulations. The Chief Accountant also maintains a liaison with representatives of the American Institute of Certified Public Accountants (AICPA), the Financial Accounting Standards Board (FASB), and others who are engaged in the development of accounting principles. (Chapter 5 focuses attention on the interaction between the SEC and the accounting profession in the development of generally accepted accounting principles).

Office of the General Counsel. The Office of the General Counsel is the chief legal office of the Commission. The responsibilities of this office are threefold:

1. To represent the Commission in judicial proceedings
2. To handle legal matters which cut across the lines of work of several operating divisions
3. To provide advice and assistance to the Commission, its operating divisions, and regional offices with respect to statutory interpretation, rule making, legislative matters, and other legal problems.[19]

In the execution of these responsibilities, General Counsel can act on its own initiative as well as at the request of the Commission. The office helps prepare reports to Congress and coordinates the preparation of any legislative proposals offered by the Commission. It also reviews all cases where criminal prosecution is recommended.

Other Offices. Other offices provide vital support for SEC activities, but their work exceeds the scope of this book. The serious student can find descriptive material in SEC publications.

---

[19] Securities and Exchange Commission, *The Work of the Securities and Exchange Commission* (Washington: U.S. Government Printing Office, 1978), p. 20.

Summary

A popular misconception is that federal securities laws resulted from the market crash of 1929 and the ensuing depression. It is true that final impetus was given to federal laws by these events, but attempts at federal control and supervision of securities markets extend to the late 19th century in this country and back as far as the 13th century in England.

Inasmuch as public financing is essential to the U.S. economy, investor confidence in securities is imperative. When confidence was shaken during the depression, restoration of public confidence was viewed as holding the key to economic recovery. The Securities Act of 1933 and the Securities Exchange Act of 1934, along with other statutes, were attempts to infuse a new spirit of trust in securities markets while protecting the public from fraudulent losses. Disclosure of pertinent information, coupled with the power to enforce the law against fraudulent acts, became the primary objective of the newly created SEC.

The SEC is organized in a manner conducive to authoritative supervision, allowing honest trading in investment securities while prohibiting deceit and manipulation. To enable the SEC to accomplish its purpose, five major operating divisions were established. These divisions are organized along functional lines with each division having responsibilities under one or more of the Securities Acts. Several staff offices lend specific, professional expertise to each of the operating divisions. Regional and branch offices are involved in the investigative activities of the Commission, but they also provide an effective network for receiving and disseminating important information.

A closer look at the laws administered by the SEC comprises the next chapter.

DISCUSSION QUESTIONS

1. How did businesses evolve into a state where external disclosure of financial information became necessary?

2. Was securities legislation in the 1930s the first attempt at regulation of capital markets?

3. What are blue-sky laws? Explain the major categories of these laws. Have they been effective in regulating securities? Why or why not?

4. List the practices during the 1920s that led to the erosion of the stock market. Explain why those practices had such a negative effect.

5. What is the primary function of the SEC? Explain.

6. Some individuals view the establishment of the SEC as unnecessary and unproductive. Do you agree or disagree? Why?

7. What degree of influence does the SEC have in the securities markets? What role do you see the SEC taking in relation to the securities markets during the next decade?

8. Describe the general characteristics of the organization of the SEC. Identify each of the divisions and explain the major purpose and function of each.

9. Explain the activities and the importance of the regional offices.

10. What is the role of the Chief Accountant? Why is this role so important to the accounting profession?

CHAPTER 2

LEGAL FRAMEWORK OF THE SEC

Since the SEC functions with the authority of law, attention must be given to the Acts constituting the legal basis from which the Commission operates. Chapter 2 presents a brief introduction of each of the several Acts involved to give the reader an appreciation for the scope of authority of the SEC. While the chapter does not provide great detail, sufficient exposure is given so that the most relevant portions of each Act can be properly examined and explained.

The SEC's legal framework is important to the accountant and business executive since each has a vital role, both statutory and assumed, under several of the Acts. Further, the past several years have seen a proliferation of securities available to investors. Each issue is supported by extensive financial reports, many of which are certified by public accountants. As the number of securities issued and traded has increased, accountants and business people have played an important role in the securities market. The changing and expanding SEC reporting requirements demand the constant attention of accountants and business people. Students of accounting and business must, therefore, be aware of the basic laws governing the SEC and of the empowering Acts of the SEC. This chapter and Chapter 3, which presents an overview of the registration process, are of real importance to the business student.

The stated purpose of the Commission—to provide "full and fair" disclosure to investors—is summarized in the following statement by the SEC:

> Congress, in enacting the Federal Securities Laws, created a continuous disclosure system designed to protect investors and to assure the maintenance of fair and honest securities markets. The Commission, in administering and implementing these laws, has sought to coordinate and integrate this disclosure system. . . . The legislative history of the Se-

curities Act of 1933 indicates that the main concern of Congress was to provide full and fair disclosure in connection with the offer and sale of securities.[1]

The various Acts also give the Commission the authority to regulate problem areas in the economy in the interest of consumers in general.

Primary Acts

The primary Acts administered by the SEC are the Securities Act of 1933 and the Securities Exchange Act of 1934. Both Acts have been revised through amendments, and the emphasis on disclosure has been increased. The major efforts of accounting-related SEC business are controlled by these two Acts and by the forms and disclosures they require.

Securities Act of 1933

The first of the securities laws passed under Roosevelt's New Deal was the Securities Act of 1933. This Act was designed to protect investors from the false claims that had existed prior to the stock market crash in 1929. The purpose of the 1933 Act is to regulate the initial offering for sale and the actual sale of securities using the mail system (interstate commerce) for offers or distribution. The 1933 Act does not concern itself with the trading of securities after their initial distribution.

Objectives of the 1933 Act. The Securities Act of 1933, often referred to as the "truth in securities" law, has two basic objectives: "(a) to provide investors with material financial and other information concerning securities offered for public sale; and (b) to prohibit misrepresentation, deceit, and other fraudulent acts and practices in the sale of securities generally (whether or not required to be registered)."[2]

The first objective is an attempt to ensure that investors are given full and fair disclosure of all pertinent information about a firm. This objective is accomplished by the requirement that any firm offering securities for public sale, except those specifically exempted, must file a registration statement with the Commission and provide potential investors with a prospectus that contains most, but not all, of the information

---

[1] The Securities and Exchange Commission, *SEC Docket* (Vol. 4, No. 5, May 7, 1974), p. 155.

[2] The Securities and Exchange Commission, *The Work of the Securities and Exchange Commission* (Washington: U.S. Government Printing Office, 1978), p. 1.

given to the SEC. The law assumes, rightly or wrongly, that the disclosure of information concerning the issue and the offering will allow an investor to make an informed choice among alternative investments.

Such stringent registration requirements do not prohibit speculative securities from entering the market, nor do they guarantee against losses. The required disclosures do allow an investor, however, to examine investment possibilities more carefully.

While it is not the purpose of the 1933 Act or the SEC to judge the merits of securities offered for sale, the SEC does, through its strict disclosure and reporting requirements, determine if the registration statement and the prospectus are deficient. (The type and extent of SEC reviews are explained in Chapter 3.) The intent of the law is that "the Government should not take the responsibility for determining the investor's choice among investment opportunities but should make certain the investor has an opportunity to make such choice on the basis of full disclosure of the pertinent facts and in the absence of fraud." [3] Thus, the 1933 Act is a "disclosure" statute. Disclosures are provided by means of a registration statement and a prospectus, each of which contains relevant financial and other information.

Registration itself does not guarantee the accuracy of the registration statement or the prospectus. Severe penalties for false or misleading information promote the implementation of the second objective of this Act and encourage the issuer to provide information that is complete, accurate, and honest. The 1933 Act also provides for the right of an investor to recover, through state or federal courts, any losses incurred as a result of false or misleading registrations and prospectuses. Section 11 of the 1933 Act states that anyone connected with the registration statement, including accountants, is liable for the accuracy of the statements. (Chapter 5 discusses the liability of managers and accountants under the various Acts.)

As securities have been issued more frequently and for greater amounts, there appears to have been an increase in the number of court proceedings for fraudulent practices or negligence in the sale of securities. The *Wall Street Journal* and other publications, as well as SEC publications, almost daily contain reference to such actions. Many of the litigations involve accounting firms which audit the financial statements for an issuer or involve other individuals who are in some other way associated with the fraudulent presentations. Fair and full disclosure is

[3] Hamer H. Budge, statement before Subcommittee on Antitrust and Monopoly of Senate Committees on the Judiciary (February 18, 1970). Budge is a former Chairman of the SEC.

the objective, and the SEC insists that companies comply or penalties will be imposed.

Not all securities listed for sale must be registered with the Commission. The 1933 Act provides for certain exemptions, namely:

(1) private offerings to a limited number of persons or institutions who have access to the kind of information registration would disclose and who do not propose to redistribute the securities, (2) offerings restricted to the residents of the State in which the issuing company is organized and doing business, (3) securities of municipal, State, Federal and other governmental instrumentalities, of charitable institutions, of banks, and of carriers subject to the Interstate Commerce Act, (4) offerings not in excess of certain specified amounts made in compliance with regulations of the Commission . . . (5) offerings of "small business investment companies" made in accordance with rules and regulations of the Commission.[4]

Exemptions may be divided into two categories: (1) exempt securities, and (2) exempt transactions. Examples of securities which are exempt are those offered by banks, nonprofit organizations, governments, and common carriers. Also exempt are *intrastate* offerings of securities. The primary exempt transactions are private offerings [see (1) in above quotation].[5] It should be noted that these exemptions are from the registration requirements; they do not decrease the liability imposed by the Act.

In addition to the examples of exemptions mentioned, the Commission has the authority under Section 3 (b) of the 1933 Act to exempt other offerings when the amount of capital to be raised is small and the public offering limited. Congress and the SEC have approved an increase from $500,000 to $1,500,000 as the maximum amount that can be raised in a public offering without registration. Exemptions in this category must still comply with certain rules and regulations of the Commission. A Regulation A offering is the most common example of this type and is referred to as a "small issue exemption."

Although exempt from registration, Regulation A offerings do require the use of an offering circular, similar to a prospectus, containing financial and other information. Audited financial statements may be required. The notification of the SEC and the filing of information is also required. Actually, the procedures are very similar to registration, but the disclosure requirements are not as extensive. The filings are received

---

[4] The Securities and Exchange Commission, *The Work of the Securities and Exchange Commission*, p. 2.

[5] For additional detail, see Section 3 and Section 4 of the Securities Act of 1933.

and reviewed by SEC regional offices in a manner similar to that used by the SEC's main office in Washington, D.C. for registration statements. Comments are generally received from the regional SEC offices, and notice of no further comments from a regional office indicates that the Regulation A offering may become effective.

Effect on Accountants. Among the most important information contained in a registration statement and prospectus are the financial statements and supporting schedules, most of which must be certified by an independent public accountant. The certification must be a manually signed document accompanying the registration statement. The preparation and auditing of these financial reports in the manner required is a tedious yet important job, and it is the principal work done by accountants under the 1933 Act.

Other work incidental to but not required by the 1933 Act includes the issuance of a "comfort letter" by an independent accountant. The underwriter of an issue has an obligation to exercise "due diligence" to verify the accuracy of the registration statement itself as well as any unaudited, interim statements included to update the certified statements. The comfort letter from the company's independent accountant to the underwriter and legal counsel gives negative assurance on the unaudited financial statements of the issuer; i.e., the letter states that the reviewing accountant has found no indication that the statements are false or misleading. The accountant does not generally perform an audit of the interim statements but does make a limited review of the statements and supporting information. The comfort letter is not a requirement of the 1933 Act and is not filed with the SEC, but it is generally requested by the underwriter as evidence that due diligence has been exercised concerning the reliability of the prospectus.[6]

Comfort letters are generally furnished pursuant to an underwriter's agreement and refer to one or more of the following subjects: (1) the independence of the accountants; (2) a statement of compliance as to form in all material respects of the audited financial statements and schedules required by the registration of securities under the Securities Act; (3) reference to the unaudited statements and their reasonableness;

---

[6] See AICPA Committee on Auditing Procedure, *Statement on Auditing Procedure*, Publication No. 48 (New York: American Institute of Certified Public Accountants, 1971). This statement explains the comfort letter and gives the opinion of the Committee on Auditing Procedures regarding its use, form, and application. See also *Statement on Auditing Standards*, Nos. 10 and 13 (New York: American Institute of Certified Public Accountants, December, 1975, and May, 1976, respectively). These statements offer guidelines for the limited review of interim financial information.

and (4) reference to significant changes in financial items since the date of the audited statements. Accountants may also be asked to comment on tables, statistics, and other financial information in the registration statement but should be careful not to go beyond their areas of expertise in giving comfort. Generally, the comfort letter will conclude with an explicit statement indicating that the letter is for use solely by the underwriters and is not to be filed as a part of the registration statement.

Another important function of the accountant is providing assistance in preparing, reviewing, and submitting the financial statements and supporting schedules required in a registration statement. This function is discussed in more detail in Chapter 3.

Securities Exchange Act of 1934

Soon after passing the Securities Act of 1933, Congress moved to regulate the trading of securities on secondary markets through brokers and exchanges and to eliminate certain abuses in the trading of securities after their initial distribution. Congress also realized the necessity of having an organization designed specifically to carry out the function described in the laws it was considering. Thus, it was with the Securities Exchange Act of 1934 that the SEC came into being.

In general, the 1934 Act is a statement of all the authority needed to successfully regulate securities trading on the national exchanges. Unlike the 1933 Act, which restricts itself primarily to initial offerings, the 1934 Act is concerned with several aspects of securities trading. The 1934 Act initially extended the full and fair disclosure doctrine to include all companies that had securities registered on the national securities exchanges. In 1964, the Securities Act Amendments extended the disclosure requirement to the securities of companies which trade on over-the-counter markets. This requirement is limited, however, to companies having over $1 million in assets and 500 or more stockholders.

Registration of Securities Issuers. Section 12 (a) of the 1934 Act states that companies desiring to have their securities traded on any of the national exchanges must file a registration statement quite similar to, although not as extensive as, the one required by the 1933 Act. This registration requirement is now extended to include over-the-counter markets, except for the securities of small companies under the size limitations mentioned above. It must be understood that the 1933 and 1934 Acts are independent of each other, and registration under one does not meet the requirement of the other. A prospectus is not required by the 1934 Act because trading on secondary markets is open to everyone, and companies cannot determine who might be interested in their securities.

In addition to the registration of outstanding securities and the disclosures involved in that process, the 1934 Act requires updated information to be filed with the Commission by means of periodic reports. The annual report to the SEC (Form 10-K) and the quarterly reports (Form 10-Q) are the most widely known and used. All of this information, with certain limited exceptions, is public information and is available at the offices of the SEC, investment banking firms, and the securities exchanges. While it is difficult to measure the exact benefits of the 1934 Act disclosures, for most major U.S. companies the costs and time involved in complying with the continuous reporting requirements of the 1934 Act are significant.

As in the case of the 1933 Act, registration and continued reporting do not guarantee accuracy. However, the SEC can file court proceedings against those who prepare and file (or are associated with the filing of) fraudulent reports and can suspend the trading in securities of companies that fail to make full and accurate reports or repeatedly fail to file on a timely basis.

Registration of Exchanges and Brokers. Another important aspect of the 1934 Act is the requirement that national securities exchanges be registered. In its application for registration, a national exchange must file with the Commission a report giving comprehensive data concerning the rules of the exchange and the scope of its operations. The exchange must also agree to comply with the requirements of the 1934 Act and to enforce compliance by the brokers who are members of the exchange. The application will be approved if the SEC feels the exchange is organized in a manner that will allow it to adhere to the requirements of the law. The disclosures subsequently required of exchanges allow the Commission to monitor their activities continuously.

Brokers dealing in over-the-counter markets are also required to register with the SEC. (Brokers who deal only in intrastate sales are exempt from this registration requirement.) The Commission has specified that registered brokers and dealers must submit periodic reports and records of transactions, and it has established minimum capital requirements for brokers. An extensive revision of these requirements was made in Accounting Series Release (ASR) No. 156, dated April 26, 1974. This release specifies the ledgers, accounts, and journals that must be kept and the maximum number of days that can elapse between any transaction and the posting or recording of that transaction.

Protection of Investors. The 1934 Act contains other measures designed to provide fair securities markets for the investor. The law prohibits the use of any "manipulative or deceptive device or contrivance" [Section 10(b)]. The 1934 Act specifically forbids such practices as wash sales and matched orders (where buy and sell orders are made in rapid succession in order to give the impression of active trading), induced trading by false statements, misuse of pro forma financial statements, and certain other practices such as price stabilization and short sales. In general, it discourages any fraudulent plot or scheme designed to manipulate the market for temporary advantage.

To further protect the investor, any officer, director, or person who owns more than 10 percent of a registered company must file an initial report with the SEC as well as the exchange where the company's securities are traded and must list any holdings of equity securities. Thereafter, a report must be filed for any month in which changes are made in the holdings. Any gains made on short-term transactions or on short sales may be recovered by the company or on its behalf by any of its security holders. This requirement discourages an "insider" from using confidential corporate information to advantage in trading equity securities. A considerable amount of litigation has been enacted relating to insider trading, with the insider almost always the loser.

Other Provisions. In regulating securities trading on the national exchanges, the 1934 Act has three other important provisions. The first is the authority to regulate proxy solicitation for the election of directors or for approval of other corporate actions. This provision is closely tied to the disclosure objective of the 1934 Act. Section 14 (a) gives very broad power to the SEC by making it unlawful for anyone to solicit a proxy or consent except under the rules the SEC may establish for the protection of investors. The purpose of the proxy rule is to ensure that sufficient disclosures are made to permit an investor to use the right to vote intelligently. These proxy requirements are probably the most effective disclosure rules in the area of securities laws.

A second provision calls for the disclosure of all pertinent information in tender offer solicitations. Before tender offers can be made, the prospective buyer must file with the SEC the following information: the principal business of the buyer, source of funds to be used in the purchase, purpose of the transaction, and the amount of equity securities to be purchased. This regulation prevents any surprise "take-over bids" and allows an issuer time to consider the tender offer.

A final provision of the 1934 Act authorizes the Board of Governors of the Federal Reserve System to control the use of margins in securities trading. Margins can be raised or lowered, depending on whether the Federal Reserve desires to stimulate or to curtail investment. The SEC retains the responsibility of enforcing the credit restrictions, which it does in connection with its periodic review of the exchanges and brokers.

Enforcement Power. The SEC is given broad enforcement powers under the 1934 Act. If the rules of operation for exchanges prove to be ineffectual in implementing the requirements of the Commission, the SEC can alter or supplement them. The SEC can suspend trading of a security for not more than 10 days (a series of orders has enabled the SEC to suspend trading for extended periods, however) and can suspend all trading on any exchange for up to 90 days. If substantive hearings show that the issuer failed to comply with the requirements of the securities laws, the Commission can delist any security. Brokers and dealers can be prevented, either temporarily or permanently, from working in the securities market; and investigations can be initiated if deemed necessary to determine violations of any of the Acts or rules administered by the SEC.

Effect on Accountants. Accountants can also be censured, and their work is subject to approval by the SEC. An accountant is involved in the preparation and review of a major portion of the reports and statements required by the 1934 Act. The financial statements in the annual report to stockholders and in the 10-K report must be certified. In addition, accountants consult and assist in the preparation of the quarterly 10-Q reports and other periodic reports, which are the result of many hours of work by both the accounting staff of the registrant and by its independent certifying accountants.

Since the SEC requires periodic reports from the brokers and dealers who are registered in the over-the-counter markets, the books of these brokers must be thoroughly audited, and extensive financial reports must be prepared and certified by an independent public accountant. With the requirements of ASR No. 156, accountants should be equipped to give expert assistance to a broker to assure that the broker meets the strict record keeping and financial reporting requirements of the SEC.

In addition to the auditing of brokers' and dealers' books, another important area of concern for the accountant is proxy statements. These statements, for the most part, must be accompanied and supported by certified financial statements. The accountant, again, is expected to provide professional expertise in the proper preparation and documentation of these statements.

Finally, a 1977 amendment to the 1934 Act will likely have an important influence on accountants. The Foreign Corrupt Practices Act amended Section 13(b) of the 1934 Act to require those companies under SEC jurisdiction to maintain proper books, records, and accounts and a sufficient system of internal control. The role of accountants in this regard is not yet defined, but their responsibility will probably be increased. The Foreign Corrupt Practices Act of 1977 is discussed later in this chapter.

Secondary Acts

In addition to the primary Acts—the Securities Act of 1933 and the Securities Exchange Act of 1934—there are secondary Acts which relate to the SEC and which are important to businesses and to the public in general. These other Acts are: The Public Utility Holding Company Act of 1935; the Trust Indenture Act of 1939; the Investment Company Act of 1940; the Investment Advisers Act of 1940; the National Bankruptcy Act, Chapter XI; the Securities Investor Protection Act of 1970; and the Foreign Corrupt Practices Act of 1977.

Public Utility Holding Company Act of 1935

Legal Requirements. The Securities and Exchange Commission states of the Public Utility Holding Company Act of 1935: "This statute was enacted by Congress to correct the many abuses which congressional inquiries had disclosed in the financing and operation of electric and gas public-utility holding-company systems."[7]

In 1928, when the Federal Trade Commission (FTC) began a thorough review of the practices and organizational structure of the utilities industry, it uncovered a system of huge utility empires controlling widely scattered subsidiaries which had little or no economical or functional relationship to each other. Such companies were pyramided together, layer upon layer, and possessed very complex capital structures developed to utilize financial leverage and to reduce the equity investment.[8]

As a regulative device given the SEC by the 1935 Act, Section 11, commonly known as the "death sentence," was initiated. The respon-

---

[7] The Securities and Exchange Commission, *The Work of the Securities and Exchange Commission*, p. 12.

[8] *Ibid.*

sibility of the SEC, according to Section 11(a) is "to determine the extent to which the corporate structure . . . may be simplified, unnecessary complexities therein eliminated, voting power fairly and equitably distributed . . . and the properties and business thereof confined to those necessary or appropriate to the operations of an integrated public utility system." The result was a geographic integration by which the SEC subdivided nearly all of the utility empires and simplified the capital structure of virtually all utility companies. The goal of the SEC was to create simple, coordinated systems confined to a single area or region and limited in such a way as not to impair the advantages of localized management, efficient operation, and effective local regulation.

The 1935 Act also empowers the SEC to regulate the terms and form of securities issued by utility companies. A reasonable capital structure is thereby maintained and competition is ensured among investment banks for underwriting and other services rendered to utility companies. As a result, the interests of both consumers and investors are protected. Investors benefit from the improved financial stability and strength, and consumers benefit from the regulation of utility company size and operation.

A registration requirement is the primary tool used to correct the abuses found in the exhaustive survey by the FTC. Registration under the 1935 Act requires companies involved in electric utility or retail gas operations to furnish to the SEC information concerning their capital structures and the nature of their businesses. Annual reports are submitted to keep the Commission up to date on the activities of registered companies. The 1935 Act also gives the SEC power to regulate the accounting systems of registered companies, to approve any acquisition or disposition of securities and assets, and to regulate intercompany transactions, such as loans and dividend payments.

Effect on Accountants. Preparation and certification of the financial statements required by this Act are important contributions of the accountant. Reports are required at the time of initial registration and, as a means of having updated information on file at the SEC, they are required each year thereafter. Financial statements prepared according to the detailed instructions of the Uniform System of Accounts for Public Utility Holding Companies and a related system, the Uniform System of Accounts for Mutual Service Companies and Subsidiary Service Companies, require special attention from the accountant. These accounting systems represent the only detailed accounting procedures which have been prescribed to date by the SEC.

Trust Indenture Act of 1939

Legal Requirements. The Trust Indenture Act of 1939 stipulates that bonds, debentures, and other debt securities offered for public sale can be issued only under a trust indenture approved by the Commission. Because some issuers had failed to provide trustees who were capable of performing adequately on their behalf, the law was passed as protection to purchasers. The Act requires a trustee to be an independent corporation (free of conflicting interest) with a minimum capitalization of $150,000. The registration form used under the 1939 Act requires an analysis of the indenture provisions and other information, allowing the SEC to rule on the capability of the trustee to serve successfully.

Effect on Accountants. There are no requirements for certification of financial data contained in annual reports under this Act, but it is desirable to have an accountant review the indenture before it becomes final, since it could contain restrictions the accountant needs to understand in order to serve a company adequately.

Investment Company Act of 1940

Legal Requirements. The Investment Company Act of 1940 resulted from a comprehensive, four-year investigation of investment companies and investment advisers. The intent of the law is to remedy and control many of the abuses uncovered in the intensive study, which was made by the SEC pursuant to the direction of Congress, and to work out a compromise between industry representatives and the SEC. This Act, which may be the most complex statute administered by the SEC, is described by the Commission as follows:

> Under this Act, the activities of companies engaged primarily in the business of investing, reinvesting, and trading in securities and whose own securities are offered and sold to and held by the investing public, are subject to certain statutory prohibitions and to Commission regulation in accordance with prescribed standards deemed necessary to protect the interests of investors and the public.[9]

Registration with the SEC is required of all companies whose business is described in the foregoing statement. Such registration is very similar to the 1933 and 1934 Acts, but registration under the 1940 Act

---

[9] *Ibid.*, pp. 16-17.

does not eliminate the requirement for registration under the preceding Acts. Additionally, disclosure of the financial condition and investment policies of the company is required; this gives the investor access to complete information concerning the activities of investment companies. All of the disclosures must be updated periodically with reports sent to the SEC.

Other provisions (1) prohibit anyone guilty of security frauds from being associated with investment companies, (2) prohibit transactions between the companies and their directors, officers, or affiliate companies without prior Commission approval, and (3) prohibit pyramids of such companies and cross-ownership of their securities or the issuance of senior securities, except under certain conditions.

The investor should not assume that the SEC supervises the investment activities of the companies and should recognize that regulation of a company does not guarantee that its securities will be a good investment. Some protection is provided, however, in that reports of company activities must be sent to stockholders at least semiannually.

Effect on Accountants. The registration statements and reports of regulated investment companies contain detailed financial statements and schedules, all of which must be certified by independent public accountants, who must be elected by stockholders or appointed by directors and ratified by stockholders. The accountant must also conduct periodic, unannounced examinations of the securities held by investment companies and report the results to the SEC. In addition to certifying financial statements, an accountant is required to furnish an opinion covering many of the items in the reports, giving "negative assurance" with respect to some of the items. This opinion is to be given only after an extensive audit of accounts and procedures.

Investment Advisers Act of 1940

Legal Requirements. The Commission states of this Act:

> This law establishes a pattern of regulation of investment advisers which is similar in many respects to Securities Exchange Act provisions governing the conduct of brokers and dealers. It requires, with certain exceptions, that persons or firms who engage for compensation in the business of advising others about their securities transactions shall register with the Commission and conform their activities to statutory standards designed to protect the interests of investors.[10]

---

[10] *Ibid.*, pp. 17-18.

The law is directed towards proper and complete disclosure of information about investment advisers, their backgrounds, business affiliation, and bases for compensation. If the proper disclosure is not made by investment advisers, the Commission has the power either to deny registration or to suspend or revoke existing registration. The SEC may initiate injunctions or recommend prosecution of advisers for willful violations of securities laws. The Commission is also empowered to issue rules defining fraudulent practices which will not be tolerated.

Effect on Accountants. While accountants are not required to certify the registration of investment advisers, they may be appropriately involved in preparing and maintaining the extensive records and accounts required by this Act. The most important work of accountants under this Act is the examination of all securities held by investment advisers on behalf of their clients. Such an examination must be made at least once during each calendar year and must be done without prior notice to the investment adviser. Conforming to the outline prescribed in ASR No. 103, the result of the examination must be reported to the SEC.

National Bankruptcy Act, Chapter XI

Legal Requirements. Chapter XI of the National Bankruptcy Act provides for corporate reorganization of financially distressed companies. The SEC participates as an adviser to the courts during proceedings in which there is substantial public investor interest. The Commission makes recommendations regarding fees, property transactions, interim distribution to security holders, and various other legal and financial questions. However, the Commission does not have authority to veto any reorganization plan, to require adoption of its recommendations, or to make decisions in bankruptcy cases.

Of primary importance is the Commission's assistance in the formulation of plans to reorganize debtor corporations. The SEC attempts to recommend reorganization which will maximize the return to the creditors and equity security holders of the corporations.

Effect on Accountants. Independent public accountants have no responsibility in any reorganization plan except as they might be serving the interest of the debtor, trustee, or other interested party.

Securities Investor Protection Act of 1970

Legal Requirements. In the past, investors have suffered sizable losses in securities markets due to the failure and financial difficulties of brokers and dealers. Congress enacted the Securities Investor Protection Act of 1970 as an amendment to the Securities Exchange Act of 1934. The 1970 Act created the Securities Investor Protection Corporation (SIPC), a nonprofit organization whose membership comprises the brokers and dealers registered under Section 15(b) of the 1934 Act and members of the national securities exchanges. Five of the seven-member board of directors are appointed by the President of the United States, one by the Secretary of the Treasury, and one by the Federal Reserve Board. Two of the seven members may not be associated with the securities industry.

The SIPC creates a fund by collecting fees from the membership. This fund is used for the protection of investors to a limit of $50,000 for each account and a maximum of $20,000 for cash claims in each account. The Commission can apply to the U.S. District Court for an order compelling the SIPC to protect its customers if the SIPC is lax in this obligation. The SIPC is required to file annual reports and financial statements with the SEC, and the Commission can make inspections of all SIPC activities. Also, the SEC has authority in connection with the bylaws and rules of the SIPC.[11]

Effect on Accountants. The accountant serves a traditional function by certification of the financial statements of the SIPC. Additionally, accountants may serve as advisers to the SIPC in the maintenance of an adequate accounting system.

Foreign Corrupt Practices Act of 1977

Legal Requirements. Effective December 19, 1977, the Foreign Corrupt Practices Act was passed by Congress to control questionable or illegal foreign payments by U.S. companies. Under provisions of the Act, all companies in the United States and their officers, directors, employees, agents, or stockholders are prohibited from bribing foreign governmental or political officials. Foreign bribery is defined as "payments, or the offering of anything of value," to foreign officials as a means of promoting business interests. "Facilitating" or "grease" payments to relatively low-level government officials are not considered corrupt practices. Examples are payments to expedite shipments through customs or to secure required permits or licenses. Such payments are not viewed as impacting on the higher level decisions to secure a contract or otherwise increase business, but to facilitate trans-

---

[11] See Louis H. Rappaport, SEC *Accounting Practice and Procedure* (3d ed; New York: Ronald Press Co., 1972), pp. 1.8-1.9.

actions not involving discretionary action. For such payments to be allowed, and not considered illegal, the foreign officials' functions must be "essentially ministerial or clerical."

A second important element of the Foreign Corrupt Practices Act of 1977 is the requirement that all public companies must (1) keep reasonably detailed records which "accurately and fairly" reflect company financial activities, and (2) devise and maintain a system of internal accounting controls sufficient, among other things, to provide reasonable assurance that transactions are properly authorized, recorded, and accounted for.[12] These two provisions are amendments to Section 13(b) of the Securities Exchange Act of 1934. Therefore, these provisions are applicable to all publicly held companies, not just those companies with foreign operations. All companies with securities registered under Section 12 of the 1934 Act and companies required to file periodic reports pursuant to Section 15(d) of the 1934 Act come under the legal requirements of the Foreign Corrupt Practices Act.

Although the record keeping and internal control provisions were intended to strengthen the antibribery provisions of the Act, the law does not limit the application of the provisions to detection or prevention of foreign bribery. Companies found guilty of making bribes, or which are otherwise not in compliance with the Act, may be subject to fines of up to $1 million; individuals may be fined a maximum of $10,000 or imprisoned up to five years, or both.

While the Act makes certain foreign corrupt practices illegal and adds new requirements with respect to accounting records and internal controls, it does not alter existing disclosure requirements of the SEC with respect to material corporate payments and practices that are questionable and illegal. ASR No. 242, dated February 16, 1978, reads in part:

> . . . registrants have a continuing obligation to disclose all material information and all information necessary to prevent other disclosures made from being misleading with respect to such transactions. Although the legality or illegality of a particular transaction is one of the factors that must be assessed in determining its materiality, other factors must also be considered. A transaction which is not unlawful under the Act may still be material to investors and therefore required to be disclosed under the federal securities laws.

There are many uncertainties concerning the Foreign Corrupt Practices Act of 1977. To mention just a few, does the law really intend a zero

---

[12] This part of the Act incorporates *Statement on Auditing Standards, No. 1*, Section 320.28 (New York: American Institute of Certified Public Accountants, 1973).

materiality criterion when it outlaws the giving of "anything of value"? When are accounting records considered "accurate and fair"? What is an adequate system of internal control? Given the fact that Congress viewed the record keeping and internal control aspects of the Act as a means of preventing and controlling foreign corrupt practices, will a violation of the accounting provisions bring legal action where foreign practices are not involved? Until such questions are answered and additional guidelines spelled out, companies should strengthen and monitor their company codes of business conduct; managements should document their systems of internal control and correct material weaknesses; and anyone associated with companies falling under the Foreign Corrupt Practices Act of 1977 should consider carefully the additional responsibilities imposed.

Effect on Accountants. The responsibility of managerial accountants to establish good accounting records and systems of internal control is not new; neither is the responsibility of independent accountants to assist in those functions and to review the internal control system as an essential part of conducting an audit. However, the Foreign Corrupt Practices Act, through the amendment to the 1934 Securities Act, subjects companies (including accountants) to civil liability and criminal prosecution under federal securities laws. This significant change increases the responsibility of both internal and independent accountants.

The major area of increased responsibility and potential liability for accountants is the evaluation of internal controls. Accountants are currently required by *Statement on Auditing Standards No. 20* to communicate to top management and the board of directors or its audit committee any material weaknesses in internal accounting controls.[13] However, this responsibility may be expanded, and accountants may be asked to offer an opinion on the adequacy of a company's internal control system. The chairman of the SEC has indicated that reporting on internal controls for public companies will be a reality in the near future. It is not clear who will assume that responsibility, but accountants will likely be involved.

In anticipation of such developments, the AICPA has under way several projects which relate to public reporting on systems of internal control. The staff of the auditing standards division has already prepared several interpretations. One interpretation recommends that ac-

---

[13] See "Required Communication of Material Weaknesses in Internal Accounting Controls," *Statement on Auditing Standards, No. 20* (New York: American Institute of Certified Public Accountants, August, 1977).

countants not issue a report offering assurance of compliance with the internal accounting control provision of the 1977 Act. Another interpretation suggests that the Act does not require the auditor to expand the scope of study and evaluation of internal control beyond the requirement of the second audit standard of field work. Still another interpretation offers guidance to auditors in complying with *Statement on Auditing Standards No. 17,* "Illegal Acts by Clients," when material weaknesses in internal control do come to the attention of the auditor. Additional interpretations and guidelines are expected both from the accounting profession and the SEC, and perhaps even from Congress.

Due to the legal and many other uncertainties, the total implications of the Foreign Corrupt Practices Act of 1977 are not yet clear. Therefore, people in business should exercise care in assessing its potentially significant impact.

Summary

The reader who has carefully reviewed this survey of laws and Acts will be amazed at the broad powers of the SEC to control the activities and to monitor the reports of the majority of business enterprises in the United States. The SEC has been applauded as one of the most effective government agencies for its ability to ensure accurate disclosure of business activity and to control the securities exchange markets in behalf of the investing public. The wide range of the SEC's activities and powers makes it an influential member of the business community. Its influence, if anything, is expanding.

DISCUSSION QUESTIONS

1. Name the Acts governed by the SEC.

2. What are the basic objectives of the Securities Act of 1933? How are these objectives being met?

3. List the major exemptions from registration under the 1933 Act, and list the categories in which they fall.

4. What is a comfort letter? Why is one issued in connection with a registration statement?

5. What did Congress attempt to do by passing the Securities Exchange Act of 1934? What agency was established by this Act?

6. Among the measures provided to protect the outside investor are certain restrictions on insiders. What are these restrictions?

7. Explain what a proxy is. What are the proxy solicitation requirements?

8. What are the purposes of the regulations covering a tender offer?

9. How does the Federal Reserve Board regulate margins? What significance does this have?

10. What disclosure tools are used under the Public Utility Holding Company Act of 1935?

11. What are the major purposes of the Investment Company Act of 1940 and the Investment Advisers Act of 1940?

12. Why is the word "Foreign" in the title "Foreign Corrupt Practices Act of 1977" somewhat misleading?

13. In terms of the accounting profession, why is the enactment of the Foreign Corrupt Practices Act of 1977 considered a significant development?

CHAPTER 3

SEC REGISTRATION, REPORTING, AND RESEARCH

In the previous chapter, each of the Acts giving the SEC its power was explained. The purpose of this chapter is to examine the process of SEC registration, including some of the reporting requirements involved. In addition, an approach to researching SEC accounting-related problems is discussed.

The rapid growth in business activity in the United States has brought a concurrent increase in the need for companies to seek capital to finance expansion. Much of this capital is obtained from public investment. The charts in Exhibit 3-1, page 38, which show the registration filings over a forty-two-year period for the 1933 Act, give an impressive picture of the magnitude of the work done by the SEC, especially during the past 10 years.

Each filing is accompanied by a myriad of documents and schedules, and proceeds through the very detailed process explained in this chapter. If the reader keeps the charts' figures in mind as the registration and review procedures unfold, a new appreciation for the task of the SEC will surely result.

The Registration Process: An Overview

In reviewing the registration process and SEC reporting requirements, it is important to keep in mind that the SEC's intent is not to judge the merits of securities offered for sale. Furthermore, the SEC's review process does not guarantee completeness or accuracy in the reports filed with the SEC. The securities laws provide for the disclosure of material financial and other information. They also impose severe penalties for presenting false and misleading information and other fraudulent acts. The SEC's role is to determine if the evidence presented

EXHIBIT 3-1

SECURITIES EFFECTIVELY REGISTERED WITH S.E.C.
1935 – 1977

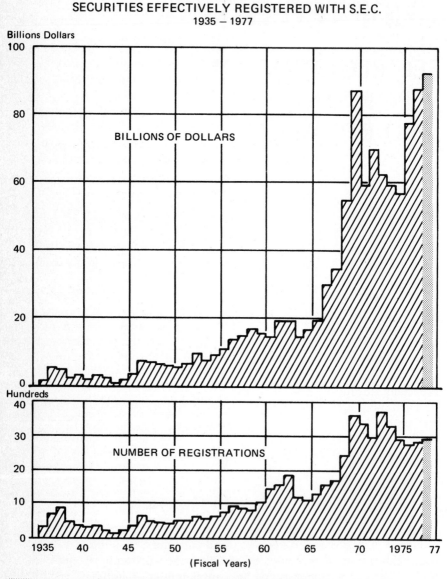

FISCAL YEAR END CHANGED FROM JUNE TO SEPTEMBER

Source: The Securities and Exchange Commission, *Annual Report of the SEC* (Washington: U.S. Government Printing Office, 1977), p. 318.

in the filed reports indicates satisfactory compliance with the applicable statutes and regulations. Any deficiencies are the responsibility of the company and the individuals involved (management, the underwriters, attorneys, accountants, etc.). The final judgment on the investment opportunity presented by the offering rests with the potential investor.

A second important point to make at the beginning of this chapter is that SEC registration involves a significant amount of effort, trauma, and expense.[1] Registration is a detailed, often lengthy process. With adequate disclosure being the main objective, registration requires simultaneous attention in several areas. Many people have seen incredible juggling acts where a performer keeps as many as seven or eight objects flying in the air by using hands, head, mouth, arms, and legs. Similarly, the registration process requires a company's management to coordinate several tasks simultaneously. Some companies are adept and successful at making registration a smooth process, while others drop one or two items, and registration becomes a nightmare of starts and stops.

Not only is the initial registration process a complicated and time-consuming task, but the continuous reporting requirements and related costs of being a "public company" may be substantial. For a public company, there are extra costs involved in preparing, printing, and distributing financial reports and proxy materials to shareholders and in the preparation and filing of SEC periodic reports (e.g., 8-K, 10-K, and 10-Q).

Extra accounting and legal work, at increased rates, are generally required for these SEC reports. There are stock exchange listing fees and transfer agent registrar fees involved. There are also additional costs related to public relations for public companies, e.g., costs associated with press releases and meetings with members of the financial community. It is also quite common to require additional personnel who become specialized in SEC matters and who make sure the SEC requirements are fulfilled. The total cost of being a public company, not counting an allocation of expense for top management's time, is estimated to be at least $35,000 to $150,000 a year.[2] For the large public companies, the costs are many times that amount. For many small companies, such costs are prohibitive.

Registration is a major part of the specific Acts administered by the SEC. With some variation due to the differing purposes of the Acts, the process under each Act is quite similar in terms of disclosure require-

---

[1] It is estimated that the average cost of filing an S-1, the form commonly used to register securities with the SEC, is now over $200,000.

[2] Jake Taylor, "Going Private," *Financial Executive* (April, 1978), p. 32.

ments and procedures. In review, the various Acts and their respective general registration requirements are:[3]

1. Securities Act of 1933: Registration of new securities offered for public sale.
2. Securities Exchange Act of 1934: Continuous reporting of publicly owned companies and registration of securities, security exchanges and certain brokers and dealers.
3. Public Utility Holding Company Act of 1935: Registration of interstate holding companies covered by this law.
4. Trust Indenture Act of 1939: Registration of trust indenture documents and supporting data.
5. Investment Company Act of 1940: Registration of investment companies.
6. Investment Advisers Act of 1940 and Securities Investor Protection Act of 1970: Registration of investment advisers.
7. Foreign Corrupt Practices Act of 1977: Affects registration only indirectly through amendment to the Securities Exchange Act of 1934; requires accurate accounting records and adequate internal accounting controls.

The focus of this chapter will be upon registration under the 1933 and 1934 Acts, the most common forms of registration involving business people and accountants. (Additional specific procedures for registration under other Acts can be found by reference to the individual Acts.)

In brief, the registration process consists of developing and filing a registration statement with the SEC. A registration statement is generally comprised of two parts, the first part containing information usually included in a prospectus. The prospectus is a rather complete booklet containing information about the company, its history, business, and the financial statements. The prospectus, described in more detail later, includes all information to be presented to prospective investors. A copy of the prospectus is customarily submitted in full satisfaction of the requirements of the first part of the registration statement. Other detailed information not included in a prospectus would be filed in the second part of the registration statement.

The Prefiling Conference

The SEC staff is available for prefiling conferences with companies having questions about registration. Such conferences often avoid

---

[3] See Leroy G. Ainsworth and Johnny S. Turner Jr., *An Overview of the SEC with a Guide to Researching Accounting-Related SEC Problems* (Provo: Brigham Young University Press, 1971), p. 11.

lengthy delays once the registration procedures have begun. In its 1948 annual report, the Commission stated:

> All members of the Commission's accounting staff are available to advise prospective registrants and their accountants in conference or by correspondence, prior to filing. Experienced practitioners who recognize unique problems regularly follow this procedure and save valuable time for themselves and their clients. The public accountant without experience with the Commission should not hesitate to do likewise.

The Commission has reiterated its policy and expanded its scope:

> The Commission has a long established policy of holding its staff available for conferences with prospective registrants or their representatives in advance of filing a registration statement. These conferences may be held for the purpose of discussing generally the problems confronting a registrant in effecting registration or to resolve specific problems of an unusual nature which are sometimes presented by involved or complicated financial transactions . . . [4]

A prefiling conference is usually held with the chief accountant of the division having jurisdiction, but unusual problems have advanced to the Office of the Chief Accountant, and even to a hearing with members of the Commission. Most inquiries, however, are resolved at the division level, and firms use this conference privilege to eliminate many roadblocks that might otherwise delay registration.

Registration Form Selection

Part of the registration process is the selection of the proper form to be used, because the SEC has designed several registration forms for use under each of the Acts. These forms contain no blanks to be filled in as do tax forms, but they are narrative in character, giving general instructions about the items of information to be furnished. Detailed information must be assembled by the companies using the form designed for the type of security being offered as well as the type of company making the offer. Louis H. Rappaport said of this procedure: "The decision as to which form to use for registration in a specific case is usually made by the company in consultation with its counsel. Since the question of which form to use is primarily a legal one, the certifying accountant should not make the decision . . . ." [5]

---

[4] "Guides for Preparation and Filing of Registration Statements," *Securities Act Release, No. 4936,* December 9, 1968.

[5] Louis H. Rappaport, *SEC Accounting Practice and Procedures* (3d ed; New York: Ronald Press Co., 1972), p. 1.17.

Registration and Reporting Under the 1933 Act

The decision to raise capital through a public offering of securities must be considered carefully. The return from the use of the proceeds must be weighed against—among other factors—the costs of registration and reporting to the SEC. Once the decision is made to "go public," the initial step is to choose the appropriate registration form. As indicated above, this is primarily a legal question. However, accountants, as well as attorneys and underwriters, should be familar with the forms used most frequently. The sections which follow contain a discussion of the more common registration forms used under the 1933 Act and the procedures for review by the SEC.

Basic Forms

Form S-1 is the most commonly used form under the 1933 Act, but there are more than 20 different forms for various types of companies and special situations. Regardless of the form used, certain information is common to all: (1) nature and history of the issuer's business; (2) its capital structure; (3) a description of any material contracts including bonus and profit-sharing arrangements; (4) a description of the securities being registered; (5) salaries and security holdings of officers and directors; (6) details of any underwriting arrangements; (7) an estimate of the net proceeds and the uses to which such proceeds will be put; and (8) detailed financial information, such as a summary of earnings, certified balance sheets, profit and loss statements, and supporting schedules.[6]

The following list of forms is not comprehensive, but it gives the major forms used for registration under the 1933 Act. Numerous additional forms of limited, specific use are supplemental to those listed here. A review of the forms will verify the earlier statement that form selection is often a difficult process. The list is in numerical order and is not grouped according to applicability to different industries.

General Description of Common 1933 Act Forms

S-1   General form for securities of all issuers for which no other form is prescribed, except that Form S-1 may not be used by foreign governments

S-2   For commercial and industrial companies in the development stage

---

[6] *Securities Regulations* (Englewood Cliffs: Prentice-Hall), p. 135, para. 118, dated November 1, 1971.

S-3   For mining corporations in the promotional stage
S-4   For closed-end management investment companies registered on
       Form N-8B-1
S-5   For open-end management investment companies registered on
       Form N-8B-1
S-6   For unit investment trusts registered on Form N-8B-2
S-7   For securities offered for cash by established companies with a
       proven history of earnings; sometimes called a "short form" be-
       cause it abbreviates the lengthy Form S-1
S-8   For securities to be offered to employees under any stock option
       or other employee benefit plan
S-10   For registration of landowner's royalty interests or rights in gas
       and oil; no financial statements required
S-11   For registration of securities of real estate investment trusts or
       other companies whose primary business is holding real estate[7]
S-13   For registration of voting trust certificates
S-14   For registration of securities acquired in mergers or consolidations
       which are to be redistributed to the public
S-16   For registration of securities to be offered on behalf of a person
       other than the registrant, to holders of convertible securities of an
       affiliate of the registrant, or to holders of outstanding warrants; a
       short form for issuers entitled to use Form S-7
S-18   A new form for registering small companies; an abbreviated S-1
       Form, available for use by companies with less than $1 million in
       assets and fewer than 500 shareholders for an initial security offer-
       ing up to $5 million
1-A   Form used to notify the SEC of an offering to be made pursuant to
       Regulation A

To give the reader an idea of the mechanics involved in registration
and the review procedures of the Commission, a summary of the process under the 1933 Act is given. Significant differences between the 1933
and 1934 Acts will be described later in this chapter, but the process is
essentially the same under any of the Acts.

Preparation of the Registration Statement

The need for coordination and cooperation really begins when the
registration statement is being prepared for filing:

The preparation of a registration statement for filing under the Securities Act of 1933 is almost invariably a combined operation. Representa-

---

[7] This form cannot be used by investment companies that are registered or must register under the Investment Company Act of 1940.

tives of the management of the registering company, the underwriters, the independent public accountants, counsel for the company, counsel for the underwriters, and, occasionally, engineers or appraisers—all have important roles in preparing the registration document.[8]

Compiling all of the information used in registration may well occupy the time of the several people mentioned above for well over a month. Additional time will be needed to draft the information into a statement acceptable to a company's board of directors.

Anywhere from one and a half to three months may be involved in the initial preparation of the statement. The time spent is often necessary to ensure that information is complete and accurate. Harry Heller states:

> It cannot be emphasized too strongly that the accuracy and adequacy of the registration statement is ultimately the responsibility of the company and its directors, officers, underwriters, and the independent public accountants whose audit and certificate in respect of financial statements is required by the statute . . . . [9]

When the document is complete, it must be delivered to the main office of the SEC in Washington, D.C. (A branch office cannot accept a registration statement.) Three complete copies of the statement and all schedules, exhibits, and the prospectus must be submitted at the time of filing. Ten additional copies of the registration statement without the exhibits must be furnished for use by the SEC staff. The required filing fee is "1/50 of 1% of the 'maximum aggregate price' at which the securities are proposed to be offered; the minimum fee is $100." [10]

SEC Review

The review process begins when the SEC receives a completed registration statement. The statute provides that the registration statement becomes effective 20 days after it is filed. However, the effective date for the registration is usually delayed by review and amendment procedures.

Review of the Statement. A normal examination by the SEC staff consists of a review of the statement and a comparison with other information available about the issuer, the industry, and other companies in

---

[8] Rappaport, *op. cit.*, p. 7.1.

[9] Harry Heller, "Disclosure Requirements Under Federal Securities Regulations," *The Business Lawyer* (January, 1961), p. 301.

[10] *Securities Regulations* (Englewood Cliffs: Prentice-Hall), p. 138, para. 124, dated April 22, 1970.

the industry. This review is made by the Division of Corporation Finance. A branch chief gives a copy of the registration statement to an analyst, an attorney, and an accountant. The analyst reviews for proper form and other nonfinancial information, while the attorney examines the legal aspects and the accountant reviews the financial statements and schedules. The purpose of this examination, as was stated earlier, is to determine compliance with applicable statutes and regulations. The staff of the SEC will try to determine if there is any materially untrue, incomplete, or misleading information in the registration statement; that is, if there is any lack of "full and fair" disclosure. However, this review does not absolve the company or anyone associated with the statement from liability under the securities laws.

Memoranda are submitted by each of the three staff experts to the branch chief. A "letter of comments," sometimes known as a "deficiency letter," is then prepared and sent to the company. This letter outlines the deficiencies that the staff has found in the registration statement and makes suggestions for improvements in the document. Excerpts from a comments letter in connection with an S-1 filing are provided on pages 46 through 48 as Exhibit 3-2. This exhibit illustrates the types of comments, suggestions, and additional information requirements resulting from the SEC's review.

The comments letter, which is not part of the public record, is sent to the registrant as soon as possible so that amendments may be made or other appropriate action may be taken. The letter of comments does not delay the effective date of the registration but if corrections cannot be made within 20 days, the SEC usually asks the issuer to file a delaying amendment. The submission of any amendment usually renews the 20-day waiting period.

Alternatives Available to SEC for Noncompliance. If a firm does not make an attempt to amend its original document, the SEC has three possible courses of action. The first is to let the statement become effective in a deficient manner, knowing the company will be liable for any actions resulting from misleading information. However, since its goal is to protect the investor, the SEC is generally not willing to let a deficient statement become effective. Furthermore, companies would rather not be the object of lawsuits for their own deficiencies.

The second action the SEC can take is to issue a refusal order. In a refusal order, the SEC must notify an issuer of defects within ten days after the filing date and a hearing must be held sometime during the next ten days to allow for correction. Because of the time pressures and lags involved, this action has been used sparingly by the SEC.

EXHIBIT 3-2

LETTER OF COMMENTS

Dear _____ :

We have the following comments on the referenced registration statement.

PROSPECTUS

Prospectus Summary - page 3

There should be an appropriate cross-reference to the discussion of litigation on page 22.

Use of Proceeds and Capital Expenditures - pages 4-5

Please advise the staff (as supplemental information prior to filing an amendment) as to the status of efforts to secure financing for construction of the new plant facility.... We may have additional comments upon receipt of this information.

Capitalization - page 6

The information presented hereunder should be as of a date within 90 days of the filing date.

Statement of Earnings - pages 7-8

Three months unaudited interim results should be presented hereunder, with comparable 19-- first and last quarter data.

The presentation of interim results should be accompanied by management's discussion and analysis of such results and appropriate representations about unaudited data.

Upon requesting acceleration please provide the staff with a letter stating that there has been no adverse trend in the financial and/or operating condition of the registrant since the date of the most recent financial data presented in the prospectus. This should be signed by an authorized officer of the registrant.

To the extent that it is material, indicate the amount of the increase in net sales in 19-- and 19-- attributable to increased unit sales.

It appears that the interim results for the first quarter of the current fiscal year and the preceding fiscal year were less favorable than for the preceding quarter, namely the fourth quarter. Accordingly, there should be a discussion of this trend as part of management's analysis of the summary of operations, indicating the reasons for this trend and the likelihood of its continuing into the future.

Business - pages 11-15

Reference is made to the first two paragraphs appearing under the caption "Patents," page 14. Therein the words "covering," "covers," "cover," and "pending" should be deleted. Words such as "relating to," "applying to," "pertaining to," etc., and "filed" or "on file" may be used as applicable.

Business - Competition and Business Conditions - page 15

The registrant's position in the industry should be more precisely stated. Source documents should be identified. If the registrant is not a significant factor in the ... industry it should be so stated.

EXHIBIT 3-2 Continued

The last sentence hereunder should be supported or deleted.

Business - General - page 15

If material, discuss the effect of compliance with environmental laws and regulations. See instruction 5 to item 9 of Form S-1 as amended by Securities Act Release No. 5704 (May 5, 1976).

We wish to be advised whether or not the sales to _____ Company and _____ Company are pursuant to a contract. If so, such contract should be filed as an exhibit to the registration statement.

Principal Shareholders - page 19

An additional column should be given to the table to disclose the percent of class held by those listed after the offering is consummated, assuming the over-allotment option is exercised.

Stock Options - pages 19-20

The information presented hereunder should be as of a date within 30 days of the date of the filing.

State the number of shares which may be issued pursuant to nonqualified options.

Litigation - page 22

Reconcile the amount of damages stated in the Form 10-K (in excess of $1,000,000) with damages "in excess of $500,000" stated in the prospectus.

Counsel referred to in the last paragraph hereunder should be named and the consent of counsel should be provided.

State whether an adverse decision would have a materially adverse effect on the financial position or operations of the registrant. Please provide the staff with copies of all of the pleadings in the litigation.

In this regard, it appears that a report on Form 8-K, for May 19--, should have been filed.

Financial Statements

Pro forma earnings per share should be shown for fiscal 19-- on the face of the statements of earnings, giving recognition to the number of shares of the proposed sale of common stock, the proceeds from which will be used to retire debt. A note to the caption should explain the computation. See paragraph 23 of APB Opinion No. 15.

A reconciliation should be provided between the equity in the income (loss) of the Canadian affiliate per the statements of earnings and the amounts presented in Note 11 and the statement of changes in financial position.

The income tax reconciliation should reconcile the amounts reported in the statements of earnings to the statutory federal income tax rate. Also, all types of deferred taxes should be identified.

Although FASB Statement of Financial Accounting Standards No. 8 is only effective for fiscal years beginning on or after January 1, 1976, the Statement requires that financial statements before the effective date be restated, if practicable. If restatement of all periods presented is not practicable, financial statements published after the effective date should be restated for as many preceding periods as practicable, and the cumulative effect of applying the Statement to retained earnings at the beginning of the earliest period restated shall be included in determining net income of that period. It appears that

EXHIBIT 3-2 Continued

application of Statement No. 8 to your company could result in restatement of
prior period financial statements. If such is the case, and material restatements of income and/or retained earnings are expected, the staff urges an early
application of Statement No. 8. However, if such an earlier application is not
practicable, appropriate footnote disclosure should be made. The disclosure
should include an explanation of the requirement to restate 19-- and prior year's
income statements, using different practices for the translation of foreign
currencies, and should include quantification, to the extent practicable, of
the effects such new practices will have on previously reported income.

The major classes of inventories should be disclosed in Note 2. See Rule
5-02-6(a) of Regulation S-X. It is assumed that cost is not in excess of market
and it should be so stated.

In regard to demand notes, the average interest rate at the balance sheet
date and the means used (monthly, daily, etc.) to compute the weighted average
interest rate for the year should be disclosed.

The unfunded past service cost of the pension plan should be disclosed in
Note 6.

It is stated in Note 4 that the company is required to maintain a compensating
bank balance of 10% of the line of credit ($1,200,000). Cash in the balance
sheet is shown as $112,399. The note should state how the cash balance meets the
compensating balance requirement.

A currently dated and manually signed consent of the independent public
accountants should be included in the amendment.

General

Your attention is directed to Guides 19, 34, 42, and 45 of the Securities
Act Release No. 4936, and to Rule 463 and Form SR.

Sincerely

Branch Chief

The final course of action is issuance of a stop order. A stop order can be issued either before or after the effective date, and it halts further consideration of the statement (if before the effective date) or stops further trading of the security (if after the effective date). As indicated in the following statement from the *Securities Regulations,* such drastic action is generally not needed since most firms reply quickly to the comments letter.

> In effect, because of the weapons outlined above, the SEC has been able to use the letter of comments to compel correction of the registration statement. In only rare instances has the SEC had to resort to the stop order; these have been mainly in cases of flagrant violations.[11]

Types of Review Procedures. As explained earlier, the number of filings under the 1933 Act has greatly increased in recent years. The SEC attempted to respond to the greater workload by streamlining the lengthy review process just outlined. In 1968, the Division of Corporation Finance adopted a new procedure for review of registration statements. These procedures were reaffirmed in 1972 by Securities Act Release No. 5231. The Division was given the latitude of selecting from four different review procedures. The type of review to be made is based on an initial evaluation of the registration statement by the Commission staff. The four review procedures are:

1. *Deferred Review:* Invoked when the registration document is so poorly prepared or presents such serious problems that further staff time is not justified. Detailed comments are not prepared, but the registrant is notified of the responsibility to proceed, withdraw, or amend. Appropriate action is recommended by the staff to the Commission if the registrant decides to proceed without taking corrective measures.
2. *Cursory Review:* Registrant is advised that only a cursory review of the statement has been made by the staff and no comments will be made. The issuer will be asked to provide letters from its chief executive officer, independent auditors, and managing underwriter, stating that all are aware of the review made and of their statutory responsibilities under the 1933 Act. Upon receipt of such letters, the staff recommends that the statement become effective.
3. *Summary Review:* Registrant is advised that a limited review has been made of the registration statement and only comments that arise from that review are submitted to the registrant for consideration. Supplemental letters from the same individuals men-

---

[11] *Ibid.,* p. 144, para. 130, dated April 2, 1970.

tioned in the "Cursory Review" are requested, containing similar declarations. Upon receipt of the assurances and satisfactory compliance with the staff's limited comments, the statement will be declared effective.

4. *Customary Review:* The more complete accounting, financial, and legal review explained earlier is given to many registration documents.[12]

Regardless of the type of review, the burden of accurate and adequate disclosure is placed squarely on the shoulders of company management, who must assume liability for what is published in its name.

The Waiting Period

An important feature in the Securities Act of 1933 is the provision for the 20-day waiting period between filing and the date the registration becomes effective. This process can be accelerated, but with the rapid increase in number of registrations, there has been no "normal" waiting period—the effective date is almost always delayed. In 1962, when there were numerous first-time registrants, nearly three months elapsed between filing and receipt of the letter of comments. In 1965, it took only ten days for some registrations to be processed. The range is skewed to the longer time, however, which makes it even more necessary that a statement be adequately prepared. Then a company can move rapidly to take advantage of appropriate timing in a constantly changing securities environment.

Indication of Interest. A company need not sit idle during the waiting period; it can move to make an announcement of the prospective issue of securities. This can only be an announcement however, with no solicitation to buy. The *Securities Regulations* state:

> . . . during the waiting period, dealers may solicit "indications of interest" from their customers, and underwriters may solicit "indications of interest" from dealers. But the dealers cannot enter into contracts of sale, and the underwriters cannot form a selling group of dealers.[13]

An indication of interest expresses possible future intent, but it does not obligate an interested party to consummate the transaction. Under a 1954 amendment, information generally is distributed in three ways: (1) an oral communication; (2) a preliminary or "red herring" prospectus;

---

[12] The review procedures are explained in more detail in Rappaport, *op. cit.*, pp. 7.5–7.6.

[13] Securities Regulations (Englewood Cliffs: Prentice-Hall), p. 183, para. 125, dated April 22, 1970.

or (3) a "tombstone ad."

Word of mouth from an underwriter or dealer to known large investors can prove to be beneficial in stimulating investor interest in a forthcoming security issue. While oral communication may be effective for creating enthusiasm, its effects are probably not as widespread as with the other two methods.

A preliminary prospectus takes the form of the final prospectus, except that information as to the offering price, commissions to dealers, and other matters related to price are omitted. Otherwise, the same investment information must be disclosed. The name "red herring" is derived from the caption "Preliminary Prospectus" stamped in red ink across the front page, as shown in Exhibit 3-3 on page 52. A registration statement indicating that the registration has not yet become effective and that the securities may not yet be sold must also be included in print at least as prominent as that in the text of the document.

"Tombstone ads" are often seen in the *Wall Street Journal* and other business periodicals. Section 2(10) of the 1933 Act allows a circular or advertisement which lists sources from which a prospectus may be obtained and by whom orders will be executed. The name comes from the form these advertisements generally take. A typical tombstone ad is shown in Exhibit 3-4 on page 53. The tombstone ad is not a selling document, but it is used to locate potential buyers whose interest will be sufficiently aroused to obtain a prospectus and to make additional inquiry about the securities.

Other Waiting Period Activities. During the waiting period, the company must also prepare any substantive amendments or delaying amendments required by the SEC to prevent a deficient statement from becoming effective. Time pressures may become intense as management's attention is diffused to the many tasks being performed simultaneously.

Still another matter requires the attention of company management during the waiting period. The 1933 Act requires the managing underwriter to exercise due diligence to help prevent fraud by making careful inquiry into the nature of the security being underwritten. A "due diligence meeting" is called between representatives of the issuer, counsel for the issuer, independent public accountants, underwriters, counsel for the underwriter, and perhaps other professionals. Information is exchanged concerning the registration statement, and final problems are resolved at this meeting.

The Pricing Amendment. When a registration statement is filed, there is a general agreement between the issuer and the underwriter as

EXHIBIT 3-3

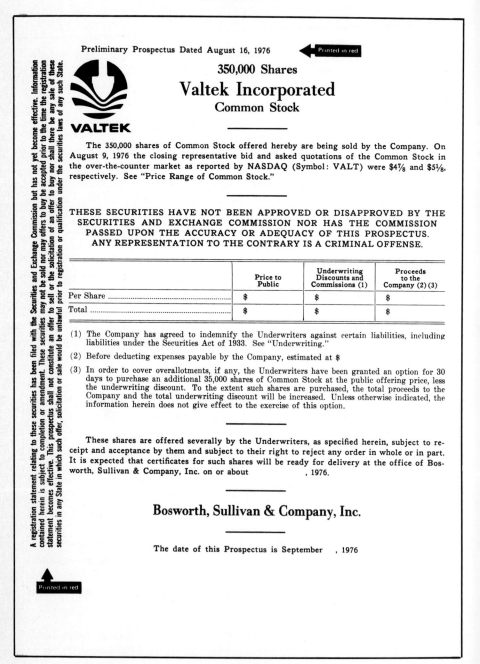

Preliminary Prospectus Dated August 16, 1976   ◀ Printed in red

350,000 Shares

Valtek Incorporated
Common Stock

VALTEK

The 350,000 shares of Common Stock offered hereby are being sold by the Company. On August 9, 1976 the closing representative bid and asked quotations of the Common Stock in the over-the-counter market as reported by NASDAQ (Symbol: VALT) were $4⅞ and $5⅛, respectively. See "Price Range of Common Stock."

THESE SECURITIES HAVE NOT BEEN APPROVED OR DISAPPROVED BY THE SECURITIES AND EXCHANGE COMMISSION NOR HAS THE COMMISSION PASSED UPON THE ACCURACY OR ADEQUACY OF THIS PROSPECTUS. ANY REPRESENTATION TO THE CONTRARY IS A CRIMINAL OFFENSE.

	Price to Public	Underwriting Discounts and Commissions (1)	Proceeds to the Company (2) (3)
Per Share	$	$	$
Total	$	$	$

(1) The Company has agreed to indemnify the Underwriters against certain liabilities, including liabilities under the Securities Act of 1933. See "Underwriting."

(2) Before deducting expenses payable by the Company, estimated at $

(3) In order to cover overallotments, if any, the Underwriters have been granted an option for 30 days to purchase an additional 35,000 shares of Common Stock at the public offering price, less the underwriting discount. To the extent such shares are purchased, the total proceeds to the Company and the total underwriting discount will be increased. Unless otherwise indicated, the information herein does not give effect to the exercise of this option.

These shares are offered severally by the Underwriters, as specified herein, subject to receipt and acceptance by them and subject to their right to reject any order in whole or in part. It is expected that certificates for such shares will be ready for delivery at the office of Bosworth, Sullivan & Company, Inc. on or about   , 1976.

Bosworth, Sullivan & Company, Inc.

The date of this Prospectus is September   , 1976

(vertical left margin text:) A registration statement relating to these securities has been filed with the Securities and Exchange Commission but has not yet become effective. Information contained herein is subject to completion or amendment. These securities may not be sold nor may offers to buy be accepted prior to the time the registration statement becomes effective. This prospectus shall not constitute an offer to sell or the solicitation of an offer to buy nor shall there be any sale of these securities in any State in which such offer, solicitation or sale would be unlawful prior to registration or qualification under the securities laws of any such State.

▲ Printed in red

EXHIBIT 3-4

TOMBSTONE AD

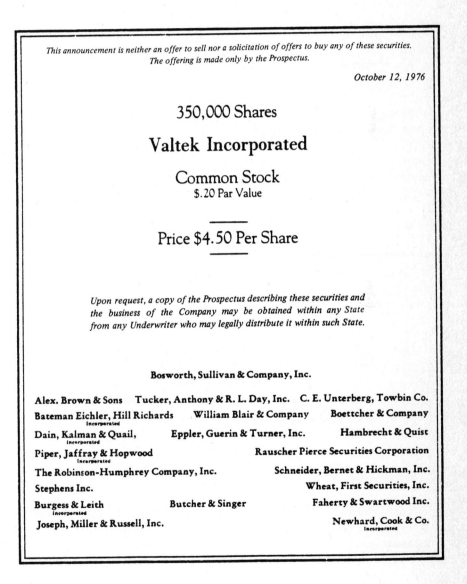

This announcement is neither an offer to sell nor a solicitation of offers to buy any of these securities. The offering is made only by the Prospectus.

October 12, 1976

350,000 Shares

Valtek Incorporated

Common Stock
$.20 Par Value

Price $4.50 Per Share

Upon request, a copy of the Prospectus describing these securities and the business of the Company may be obtained within any State from any Underwriter who may legally distribute it within such State.

Bosworth, Sullivan & Company, Inc.

Alex. Brown & Sons   **Tucker, Anthony & R. L. Day, Inc.**   **C. E. Unterberg, Towbin Co.**

Bateman Eichler, Hill Richards   **William Blair & Company**   **Boettcher & Company**
Incorporated

Dain, Kalman & Quail,   **Eppler, Guerin & Turner, Inc.**   **Hambrecht & Quist**
Incorporated

Piper, Jaffray & Hopwood   **Rauscher Pierce Securities Corporation**
Incorporated

The Robinson-Humphrey Company, Inc.   **Schneider, Bernet & Hickman, Inc.**

Stephens Inc.   **Wheat, First Securities, Inc.**

Burgess & Leith   **Butcher & Singer**   **Faherty & Swartwood Inc.**
Incorporated

Joseph, Miller & Russell, Inc.   **Newhard, Cook & Co.**
Incorporated

to the type of security being offered and the approximate amount of funds to be raised. However, the final terms relating to any interest or dividend rates, the actual price of the offering, the underwriter's discount or commission, and the net proceeds to the company have not yet been printed on the registration statement. This is accomplished by the "pricing amendment," which is generally filed at about the same time as, or perhaps just after, the "due diligence" meeting.

The pricing amendment changes only the cover page of the prospectus. To illustrate this point, compare Exhibit 3-5 on page 55, which shows the cover page of a prospectus after the pricing amendment, with Exhibit 3-3, the cover page for the preliminary prospectus. At the time of filing the pricing amendment, the registrant and underwriter usually request acceleration of the effective date of the offering. The pricing amendment is not filed until the statement is ready to become effective, and generally the effective date is within a few days of the pricing amendment.

Effective Registration Statement

Once the deficiencies have been corrected, the issuer and underwriters have properly attended to their concurrent responsibilities, and the SEC staff has informed the Commissioners that they have no significant reservations, the Commission declares the registration statement effective.[14] The issuer and underwriters are then free to proceed with the distribution and sale of the security.

With certain limited exceptions, all of the information compiled as a part of the registration statement is public information and may be inspected in the Public Reference Room of the Commission in Washington, D.C. Copies of all documents may be obtained, and prospectuses covering recent public offerings may be examined at any SEC office. There may be lengthy time lags in receiving the desired material, however.

Summary of Registration Under 1933 Act

This brief overview serves to initiate the reader to the registration detail and mechanics required by the 1933 Act. As a summary, Exhibit 3-6 on pages 56 and 57 presents a hypothetical example of the registration process. Included in the exhibit is a listing of some of the major

---

[14] As mentioned earlier, the Commission can declare a defective statement effective. However, a company would not knowingly allow that to happen, given the serious legal liability involved.

EXHIBIT 3-5

PROSPECTUS INCORPORATING PRICING AMENDMENT

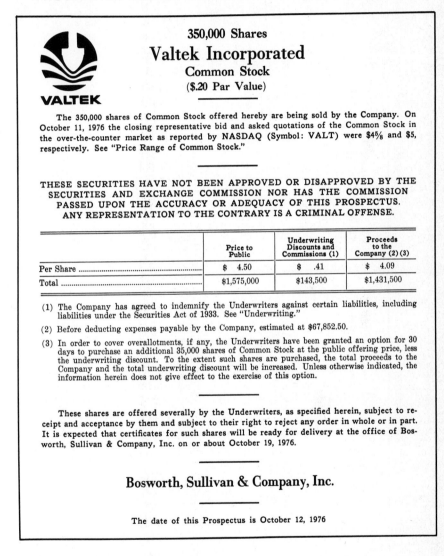

350,000 Shares

Valtek Incorporated
Common Stock
($.20 Par Value)

The 350,000 shares of Common Stock offered hereby are being sold by the Company. On October 11, 1976 the closing representative bid and asked quotations of the Common Stock in the over-the-counter market as reported by NASDAQ (Symbol: VALT) were $4⅝ and $5, respectively. See "Price Range of Common Stock."

THESE SECURITIES HAVE NOT BEEN APPROVED OR DISAPPROVED BY THE SECURITIES AND EXCHANGE COMMISSION NOR HAS THE COMMISSION PASSED UPON THE ACCURACY OR ADEQUACY OF THIS PROSPECTUS. ANY REPRESENTATION TO THE CONTRARY IS A CRIMINAL OFFENSE.

	Price to Public	Underwriting Discounts and Commissions (1)	Proceeds to the Company (2)(3)
Per Share	$ 4.50	$ .41	$ 4.09
Total	$1,575,000	$143,500	$1,431,500

(1) The Company has agreed to indemnify the Underwriters against certain liabilities, including liabilities under the Securities Act of 1933. See "Underwriting."

(2) Before deducting expenses payable by the Company, estimated at $67,852.50.

(3) In order to cover overallotments, if any, the Underwriters have been granted an option for 30 days to purchase an additional 35,000 shares of Common Stock at the public offering price, less the underwriting discount. To the extent such shares are purchased, the total proceeds to the Company and the total underwriting discount will be increased. Unless otherwise indicated, the information herein does not give effect to the exercise of this option.

These shares are offered severally by the Underwriters, as specified herein, subject to receipt and acceptance by them and subject to their right to reject any order in whole or in part. It is expected that certificates for such shares will be ready for delivery at the office of Bosworth, Sullivan & Company, Inc. on or about October 19, 1976.

Bosworth, Sullivan & Company, Inc.

The date of this Prospectus is October 12, 1976

events which must take place, an indication of the individuals involved, and some idea of the time required for a registration statement to be developed and to become effective. The other securities statutes contain similar registration procedures with variation as to content and purpose.

EXHIBIT 3-6

Illustrative Example of Registration Process

Event	Participants	Agenda	Timetable
Preliminary meeting to discuss issue	President, VP-Finance, independent accountants, underwriters, counsel	Discuss financial needs; introduce and select type of issue to meet needs.	1 July (Begin)
Form selection	Management, counsel	Select appropriate form for use in registration statement.	3 July (3 days)
Initial meeting of working group	President, VP-Finance, independent accountants, underwriter, counsel for underwriter, company counsel	Assign specific duties to each person in working group; discuss underwriting problems with this issue; discuss accounting problems with the issue.	8 July (8 days)
Second meeting of working group	Same as for initial meeting	Review work assignments; Prepare presentation to board of directors.	22 July (22 days)
Meeting of board of directors	Board of directors, members of working group	Approve proposed issue and increase of debt or equity; Authorize preparation of materials.	26 July (26 days)
Meeting of company counsel with underwriters	Company counsel, counsel for underwriters, underwriters	Discuss underwriting terms and blue sky problems.	30 July (30 days)
Meeting of working group	Members of working group	Review collected material and examine discrepancies.	6 Aug (37 days)
Prefiling conference with SEC staff	Working group members, SEC staff, other experts as needed	Review proposed registration and associated problems: legal, financial, operative.	9 Aug (40 days)
Additional meetings of working group	Members of working group	Prepare final registration statement and prospectuses.	12-30 Aug. (61 days)

Event	Participants	Task	Date
Meeting with board of directors	Board of directors, members of working group	Approve registration statement and prospectuses; discuss related topics and problems.	6 Sept. (68 days)
Meeting of working group	Members of working group	Draft final corrected registration statement.	10 Sept. (72 days)
Filing registration statement with SEC	Company counsel or representative and SEC staff	File registration statement and pay fee.	12 Sept. (74 days)
Distribution of "red herring" prospectus	Underwriters	Publicize offering.	16 Sept. (78 days)
Receipt of letter of comments	Members of working group	Relate deficiencies in registration statement.	15 Oct. (107 days)
Meeting of working group	Members of working group	Correct deficiencies and submit amendments.	21 Oct. (113 days)
"Due diligence" meeting	Management representatives, independent accountants, company counsel, underwriter's counsel, underwriters, other professionals as needed	Exchange final information and discuss pertinent problems relating to underwriting and issue.	24 Oct. (116 days)
Pricing amendment	Management, underwriters	Add the amounts for the actual price, underwriter's discount or commission, and net proceeds to company to the amended registration statement.	25 Oct. (117 days)
Notice of acceptance	SEC staff	Report from SEC staff on acceptance status of price-amended registration statement	28 Oct. (120 days)
Statement becomes effective			30 Oct. (122 days)

Registration and Reporting Under the 1934 Act

The Securities Exchange Act of 1934 was an attempt to bring together in one statute all of the necessary elements to elicit registration from the many participants in the securities market. The continuous reporting required by the 1934 Act is not designed to protect the investor against loss, but to provide "adequate and accurate disclosure of material facts."

The 1934 Act is much broader in scope than the 1933 Act. The jurisdiction of the 1934 Act includes most large and some smaller companies, stock exchanges, brokers and dealers, and national securities associations. In addition, the 1934 Act specifically prohibits manipulative devices, includes provisions for insider trading, proxy solicitations, and tender offers, and provides for "margin" requirements. The specific types of companies and the sections of the 1934 Act under which they must report periodically to the SEC include the following:

1. Companies whose securities are listed on the national securities exchanges [Section 12(b)]
2. Companies whose securities are traded over the counter, if those companies have total assets in excess of $1 million and 500 or more stockholders [Section 12 (g)]
3. Companies whose securities are traded over the counter, which do not meet the asset and stockholder tests in (2) but which have elected to voluntarily comply with the 1934 Act reporting requirements [Section 12(g)]
4. Companies with over 300 stockholders of a class of securities that are registered under the 1933 Act [Section 15(d)]

The breadth of coverage of the 1934 Act can be illustrated by considering the 1934 Act report forms.

Report Forms

Since registration and reporting requirements under the 1934 Act are very broad in coverage, there are ten separate categories of report forms:

1. Forms for registration of national securities exchanges
2. Forms for reports to be filed by officers, directors, and security holders
3. Forms for registration of securities on national securities exchanges
4. Forms for annual and other reports of issuers
5. Forms for amendments to registration statements and reports to issuers
6. Forms for registration of brokers and dealers on over-the-counter markets

7. Forms for reports by certain exchange members, brokers, and dealers
8. Forms for reports concerning stabilization
9. Forms for registration and reporting by national securities associations and affiliates
10. Forms for reports by market makers and certain other registered broker-dealers in securities traded on national securities exchanges [15]

Selection of Forms

Responsibility for selection of the appropriate forms to be used rests with the registrant and its counsel. Again to illustrate the numerous forms used, a brief description of the basic forms for categories (3) and (4) are given below, along with a list of the schedules of supporting information that must be filed. The numerical forms are for registration while the numerical-alphabetical forms are for the periodic reports associated with such prior registration—e.g., a firm registering by using Form 10 would use Form 10-K for its annual reports thereafter.

Forms—1934 Act

10	For registration of a class of securities for which no other form is specified
12	For registration of securities of an issuer who files with another federal agency (e.g., the Federal Power Commission)
14	For registration of certificates of deposit
16	For registration of voting trust certificates
18	For registration of securities of foreign governments or political subdivisions
19	For permanent registration of American certificates issued against securities of foreign issuers
20	For registration of any class of securities issued by foreign private issuers
25	For notification of removal from listing of matured or redeemed securities
26	For notification of the admission to trading of a substitute or additional class of security
BD	General registration form for all brokers and dealers
8-K	Current report required to be filed within 15 days after the

---

[15] Securities and Exchange Commission, *General Rules and Regulations Under the Securities Exchange Act of 1934* (Washington: U.S. Government Printing Office, 1970), p. 143.

occurrence of a "material" event

10-K   Annual report for which no other form is prescribed
11-K   Annual report for employee stock purchase or similar plans
12-K   Annual report form for companies using Form 12 for registration
14-K   Annual report form for issuers of certificates of deposit
16-K   Annual report form relating to voting trust certificates
18-K   Annual reports of foreign governments or political subdivisions
19-K   Annual report form for issuers of American certificates
20-K   Annual report form for foreign private issuers
7-Q   Quarterly reports of real estate investment trusts or of companies whose major business is holding real estate
10-Q   Quarterly reports containing specified financial information filed for each of the first three quarters of a company's fiscal year

Schedules

I   Marketable securities—other security
II   Amounts receivable from underwriters, promoters, directors, officers, employees, and principal holders (other than affiliates) of equity securities of the person and its affiliates
III   Investments in, equity in earnings of, and dividends received from affiliates and other persons
IV   Indebtedness of affiliates and other persons—not current
V   Property, plant, and equipment
VI   Accumulated depreciation, depletion, and amortization of property
VII   Intangible assets, deferred research and development expenses, preoperating expenses, and similar deferrals
VIII   Accumulated depreciation and amortization of intangible assets
IX   Bonds, mortgages, and similar debt
X   Indebtedness to affiliates and other persons—not current
XI   Guarantees of securities of other issuers
XII   Valuation and qualifying accounts and reserves
XIII   Capital shares
XIV   Warrants or rights
XV   Other securities
XVI   Supplementary income statement information
XVII   Real estate and accumulated depreciation
XVIII   Mortgage loans on real estate
XIX   Other investments

Differences in Registration Under the 1933 and 1934 Acts

There are several differences in the registration procedures and reporting requirements under the 1933 and 1934 Acts. The scope of the registration itself is the first such difference. The 1933 Act requires registration for all initial offerings of securities for public sale. Thus, to raise money in the primary capital market essentially requires 1933 Act registration, and a prospectus is always required. Under the 1933 Act, registration is for a specific security to be issued in a specific amount. The SEC requires a post-effective report on the sale of a new security to verify the amount sold and to cancel any excess not sold. Under the 1934 Act, however, an entire class of securities is registered with no amount specified. The registration covers the amount of the security outstanding and any additional shares of that class of security that may be issued in the future. Then, without again experiencing the difficulties of registration, a company may issue more securities. Thus, the 1934 Act deals with the secondary capital markets and no prospectus is required.

Another difference between the two Acts is the extensive reporting requirements of the 1934 Act. As securities listed under the 1934 Act are traded continuously over many years, the statute provides for continuous disclosure of company activities through annual, quarterly, and special reports. Forms 8-K for significant current events, 10-K for annual reports, and 10-Q for quarterly reports are the most widely used. (The general content of a 10-K annual report is described later.)

The annual reports are scrutinized by the staff of the SEC to insure that a policy of satisfactory financial reporting is practiced by the firms registered under the 1934 Act. Most of this material is available to the public. Reports are filed at the regional or branch office where the company has its headquarters, and information can be reviewed by the public at this office.

The extensive reporting requirements of the 1934 Act are not confined to the periodic reports mentioned above. Insider trading requirements, proxy solicitation rules, and regulation of tender offers are but a few additional examples of the broad reporting provisions of the 1934 Act. The most recent amendments are those incorporated in the Foreign Corrupt Practices Act of 1977, which was discussed in Chapter 2.

Registration Under Other Acts

Registration requirements are similar for the other Acts supervised and enforced by the SEC. Registrations are reviewed for compliance with the specific statutes, and for completeness and fairness of disclosure. Periodic reports are required by every Act except the 1933 Act and the Trust Indenture Act of 1939. These reports contain the same basic information, and practically all of this information is made public. Specific questions about the unique procedures of each Act can be answered by consulting the text of the Act itself.

Researching SEC Accounting–Related Problems

In preparing registration statements and other SEC reports, a variety of circumstances and problems will be encountered. Because of the many different situations and complexities involved, no single, simple solution is feasible. Generally, each case requires judgment and considerable research effort. However, there are some problems that are commonly encountered in the registration process, and there is an approach to solving those common problems that seems logical.

As in other problem-solving situations, the first step in researching accounting-related questions is to identify the problem in light of the facts involved. With reference to registration, the first question is the matter of what form must be used. Of particular relevance to accountants are the additional questions concerning what financial statements must be disclosed and for how many years, what portions must be audited, and what pro forma statements are required. Related questions include what accounting principles must be followed and how detailed the disclosures must be.

When the specific questions are addressed, all alternatives must be considered. Generally, the alternatives become apparent as the major sources of information are consulted.[16] These include the instructions to the forms, the "guides" to the forms, the rules and regulations of the Acts, Regulation S-X and S-K, the Accounting Series Releases and Staff Accounting Bulletins of the SEC, generally accepted accounting principles set forth by the FASB and AICPA, and perhaps even recent registration statements and SEC reports from other companies. An important point is that the reporting requirements of the SEC are not easily determined, because of a lack of codification and cross-referencing of requirements. Some real research effort is necessary in most cases to determine exactly what is required, which in turn determines essentially what alternatives exist.

After determining what is required, accountants should exercise their judgments as to proper reporting. In many instances the statutes

---

[16] The Appendix provides an annotated bibliography of the major sources of information for researching SEC accounting-related problems.

will allow little room for choice. They may specify exactly what form to use, what is to be reported, and in what manner. In many other situations, however, it will not be completely clear what is required. In those cases the accountant should use good common sense, present the strongest case possible for the position taken, and substantiate that position with complete documentation. In most cases, if the position taken is logical and well supported, the SEC will allow the reporting requested. There are many "gray" areas where such an approach is valid and will be successful when dealing with the SEC. The key is to make a strong, logical agreement that is well supported.

Summary

The many simultaneous tasks in which a company engages by seeking registration of its securities with the SEC require thorough concentration and the coordination of the activities of several experts. The registration process, as the reader must be aware, is an important undertaking for both a company and the Commission.

The registration goal of corporations is to tap public capital markets for investment funds to stay abreast of the rapidly expanding business activity in the United States. The goal and responsibility of the SEC is to protect investors by requiring full disclosure of an issuer's activities so that investors can reach informed decisions. Goal congruence is obviously not always achieved, but an integrated, cooperative system is approached by the registration and reporting processes described in this chapter.

In researching SEC accounting-related issues, accountants will need to examine carefully all relevant sources of information, including the forms, the Acts, the rules and regulations, and the interpretations of the SEC and the accounting profession. When the exact reporting requirements are not specified by law, the registrant, with the help of its accountants and other experts, should develop a logical position that is well documented. The SEC will generally accept such a position, provided it meets their "full and fair" disclosure standard. There is ample room for reasoned judgment and flexibility in working with the SEC.

DISCUSSION QUESTIONS

1. What is the overall purpose of the SEC registration and review process?
2. Briefly outline the registration process for the 1933 Act.

3. What is the policy of the SEC with respect to prefiling conferences? How should accountants advise clients to begin the registration process?

4. What information is commonly required in the basic registration forms?

5. Briefly describe the review procedure followed by the SEC staff upon receipt of the registration statement.

6. What is the purpose of a letter of comments?

7. If a registration statement is deficient, what are the courses of action the SEC may take? What are the results of these courses of action?

8. The types of review of the registration statement by the SEC were concisely set forth in 1972. List and explain these review procedures.

9. While waiting for completion of the review, what can a company do in anticipation of approval from the SEC to proceed?

10. What is a "red herring" or preliminary prospectus? What information does it contain?

11. What is a "tombstone ad"?

12. How do underwriters exercise due diligence under the 1933 Act?

13. What effect does the "pricing amendment" have on the registration statement?

14. Once a company becomes registered under the 1934 Act, to what major regulatory provisions is it subject?

15. What is a proxy?

16. For SEC purposes, what is the main distinction between pro forma and historical financial statements?

17. What are the primary differences between the requirements under the 1933 and the 1934 Acts?

18. In researching SEC accounting-related problems, what factors should be considered and what are the major sources of information to be consulted?

CHAPTER 4

AN ANALYSIS OF SEC REPORTS AND CORPORATE REPORTS

The previous chapter has examined the registration process and the forms used in that process. An appreciation for the extremely heavy workload of business corporations and the SEC divisions can be gained by multiplying by several thousand each year the procedures described. Besides handling over 4,000 new registration statements yearly, the SEC also receives quarterly, annual, and special reports from over 10,000 United States firms.

The purpose of Chapter 4 is to study examples of the registration statements and periodic reports submitted to the SEC and to compare them with corresponding reports submitted to stockholders. An initial narrative on the purpose and scope of the various financial reports is followed by comparative illustrations based on actual examples.

Reporting Responsibilities

The decision to "go public" is of great importance to any firm. Moving from private to public capital financing involves not only a major strategy shift on the part of management, but also a new emphasis on record keeping and reporting. Management must be willing to share ownership with outsiders, and must make the commitment to use the necessary resources to inform investors of corporate activities. If management is to answer for its stewardship of invested capital as well as provide for a continuation of capital flow from investor to manager, such reporting is vital.

Annual Reports

A problem arises because managements prepare two different annual reports. One report is sent to the SEC, while a separate report is given to the investor. The annual reports to the SEC are governed strictly in content and form by federal statutes, but managements have had, in the past, nearly free rein in the preparation of their annual reports to stockholders.

For years the SEC has urged managements to make the annual report to stockholders reflect more carefully the extensive disclosure requirements of reports sent to the Commission. Due to the variety of people using stockholders' reports, managements generally have been slow to respond to this request. Individuals from top management to labor unions, from homemakers to investment analysts, use annual reports to stockholders and rely on the information contained therein. The disparity between audiences presents a real problem for managements in the preparation of the annual report, a problem synthesized quite well in the following statement:

> It is not unlike an effort to write for a medical journal an article on advanced techniques in handling compound fractures that is instructive to a practicing physician, and, at the same time, is useful to a Boy Scout working to earn his merit badge in first aid.[1]

A rather simple answer is to structure the annual report to satisfy the average stockholder and let the experts utilize supplemental sources of information, such as the SEC reports. (Remember that most SEC reports are available to the public, but usually only investment analysts have taken the time to avail themselves of this information.) This solution, as indicated later, has not been adopted, probably because a simple answer does not often solve a complex problem.

Historically, the Commission has exerted some influence on the contents of the stockholders' annual reports. This influence is related to the provisions of the Securities Exchange Act of 1934 dealing with proxy statements. If a proxy solicitation is made on behalf of management in conjunction with an annual meeting where directors are to be elected, the proxy statement must be accompanied by an annual report. This allows the SEC some control over corporate information sent to stockholders, since the annual report must contain certified financial statements and other specific items of disclosure.[2]

In the author's opinion, there has been an improvement in corporate reporting in the United States during the last 40 years. Corporate managements and public accountants have made significant contributions in bringing corporate reports up to their present standards, but the SEC

---

[1] Donald P. Jones, "Management Freedom in Annual Reports," *Financial Executive* (August, 1971), p. 24.
[2] See Section 14 of the 1934 Act.

and the securities exchanges must also be given some of the credit for promoting needed improvement. To illustrate the improvements, consider the following quotes taken from annual reports. The first is from a 1902 annual report to shareholders.

> The settled plan of the directors has been to withhold all information from stockholders and others that is not called for by the stockholders in a body. So far no request for information has been made in the manner prescribed by the directors . . . [3]

The second quote is from the 1973 annual report to stockholders of a large manufacturing firm. The firm included in its stockholders' report substantially all of the information in the annual report submitted to the SEC. The company introduced the report by stating:

> This form, filed each year by all publicly owned companies, contains more detailed information than is given in the typical annual report. Our intention in presenting it here is to give all present and prospective shareholders a comprehensive picture of the firm's business and financial condition. [4]

The third quote is from the 1978 annual report of General Motors.

> The following financial statements of General Motors Corporation and Consolidated Subsidiaries were prepared by the management, which is responsible for their integrity and objectivity. The statements have been prepared in conformity with generally accepted accounting principles and, as such, include amounts based on judgments of management.
>
> Management is further responsible for maintaining a system of internal controls, including internal accounting controls, that contains organizational arrangements that provide an appropriate division of responsibility and is designed to assure that the books and records reflect the transactions of the companies and that its established policies and procedures are carefully followed. The system is constantly reviewed for its effectiveness and is augmented by written policies and guidelines, a strong program of internal audit, and the careful selection and training of qualified personnel. [5]

Additional Disclosure Requirements

The trend toward disclosing more information in the annual reports to stockholders has been prompted by amendments to the rules cover-

---

[3] Quoted in Jones, *op. cit.*, p. 23. See also Louis H. Rappaport, SEC *Accounting Practice and Procedure* (3d ed.; New York: Ronald Press Co., 1972), pp. 3.4-3.5.

[4] Teradyne, Inc., 1973 *Annual Report.*

[5] General Motors, *1978 Annual Report.*

ing proxy statements (Rules 14a-3, 14c-3, and 14c-7 of the 1934 Act). As nearly all corporations use their annual reports with proxy solicitations, the SEC has substantially increased its authority over corporate reporting. The purposes of these increasing SEC regulations are (1) to require disclosure of more meaningful information in the annual reports while giving managements the discretion of format and (2) to improve the dissemination of the more technical 10-K or 12-K reports filed with the SEC.

Essentially, the SEC disclosure requirements for a company's annual reports are: [6]

1. Audited financial statements for the last two fiscal years
2. Summary of earnings (or operations) for the last five fiscal years and a management analysis thereof
3. A brief description of the business
4. A line-of-business or product-line report for the last five fiscal years
5. Identification of directors and executive officers with the principal occupation and employer of each
6. Identification of the principal market in which the securities of the firm are traded
7. Range of market prices and dividends for each quarter of the two most recent fiscal years

An additional requirement states that, upon written request, stockholders will be furnished a free copy of the 10-K report. A reasonable charge may be made for copies of any exhibits accompanying the 10-K report.

These reporting requirements will tend to reduce the differences between annual reports to stockholders and the annual reports filed with the SEC. Investors will be increasingly exposed to technical information in annual reports and will need to become more sophisticated in their abilities to interpret the information provided.

Comparison of SEC and Corporate Reports

Attention will now be given to a comparison between corporate reports to stockholders and those filed with the SEC.

Overview

Of the numerous forms available for reporting to the SEC (see Chapter 3), only the most commonly used forms will be discussed here.

---

[6] Securities Exchange Act of 1934, *Release No. 11079* (October 31, 1974).

Excerpts from the reports of Valtek Incorporated will serve as a model. The illustrations provide contrasts for purposes of instruction and serve as useful examples of corporate reporting. Because of continuous changes in reporting standards (established by the FASB, CASB, SEC, and other regulatory agencies), the content of these examples may not completely reflect current requirements. However, the general approach is indicative of the type of disclosure presented in the reports.

The reader is reminded that the forms sent to the SEC are mostly narrative reports accompanied by financial statements and schedules. Managements are responsible for the preparation of the reports, and independent public accountants attest to the financial statements. Each form used in reporting to the SEC has varying requirements as to financial data. The most common forms are:

1. Form S-1, used for the majority of registrations pursuant to the 1933 Act

2. Proxy statements, used in conjunction with proxy solicitations for the periodic meetings of stockholders

3. Form 8-K, used by firms to report any significant event affecting the company

4. Form 10-K, the primary form for yearly reports under the 1934 Act

5. Form 10-Q, used by firms to report quarterly operations under the 1934 Act

Form 8-K does not generally require certified financial data. The information provided is mostly narrative and is intended to keep prospective shareholders (and the SEC) informed on current events that have a major effect on the company. In Exhibit 4-1 on pages 70 and 71, the financial data and certification requirements of the other four forms and the annual report to shareholders are given. This is by no means an exhaustive list of forms and statements, but gives the reader a comparative basis upon which to examine the differences and similarities between commonly used reports.

Registration Under the 1933 Act

Form S-1 is the most commonly used form when a firm wishes to register a security for issue in the primary market. The form is divided into two parts. Part I consists of information that is to be included in the prospectus, and Part II is additional information that is submitted as

EXHIBIT 4-1

Registrant's Statements	S-1		Proxy¹		10-K		10-Q²		Annual Report³	
	Years	Certified	Years	Certified	Years	Certified	Years	Certified	Years	Certified
Unconsolidated Balance Sheet⁴	1	Yes	Not required		2	Yes	Not required		Not required	
Unconsolidated Income Statement	3	Yes	Not required		2	Yes	Not required		Not required	
Unconsolidated Stockholders Equity	3	Yes	Not required		2	Yes	Not required		Not required	
Unconsolidated Changes in Financial Position	3	Yes	Not required		2	Yes	Not required		Not required	
Consolidated Balance Sheet	1	Yes	1	Yes	1	Yes	Current quarter for two years		2	Yes
Consolidated Income Statement	3	Yes	3	Yes	5	Most recent 2 years	Current quarter & year to date / 2	No	2	Yes
Consolidated Stockholders Equity	3	Yes	3	Yes	5	Most recent 2 years	Current quarter / 2	No	2	Yes
Consolidated Changes in Financial Position	3	Yes	3	Yes	2	Yes	Year to date / 2	No	2	Yes
Summary of Earnings⁵	5	No	5	No	5	No	Narrative analysis of operating results		5	No

Summarized Profit and Loss 6	As appropriate	Not required	Not required	Interim quarters	No	Not required
Summarized Capitalization and Equity	Not required	Not required	Not required	Interim quarters	No	Not required
Schedules 7	As appropriate	Schedule XVI only	As appropriate	Not required	Not required	Not required

Notes:

1. Proxy statements require financials only when used for mergers, consolidations, acquisitions, or a change in securities issued. A narrative statement, accompanied by the annual report to stockholders, is sufficient for recurring annual stockholder meetings under most circumstances.

2. ASR No. 177 and ASR No. 206 revised Form 10-Q. A subsequent release (No. 33-5579) revised the accountant's specified limited review procedures and certification requirements.

3. SEC control over annual reports comes in conjunction with proxy statement requirements. Exchange Act Release No. 11079 has substantially increased SEC authority over corporate reports.

4. All unconsolidated statements require special attention. For Form S-1 if the registration has 85 percent of consolidated sales and assets, or the subsidiary is "totally held" (defined as substantially all equity held by parent but need not be 100 percent), unconsolidated statements are not needed. For Form 10-K, if the registrant is an operating company (as opposed to a holding company) or the registrant has 75 percent of consolidated assets and gross revenues, unconsolidated statements are not needed. This is a complex area, and the SEC procedures play an important part in determining when parent consolidated financial statements are included.

5. The Summary must cover at least five years, more if clarification is needed. The Summary need not be certified, but most underwriters require certification; and the SEC needs substantial reason when certification is not given. Predominant practice is to include a complete Income Statement which satisfies the requirements for both the Summary of Earnings and Consolidated Income Statements.

6. Summarized Profit and Loss and Capitalization and Equity Statements are comparisons of the interim quarters since the fiscal year with the corresponding periods of the preceding year. Also, summarized quarterly operating data for the two most recent fiscal years must be disclosed in a footnote to the annual audited statements in SEC filings for most large companies.

7. There are 19 schedules used, but differing circumstances will require different schedules. No one firm would likely have to include all of the schedules in one year. For a list of the schedules refer to Chapter 3.

required. A general description of the items required in Parts I and II is given below. Not all items will appear in every registration statement because some items are mutually exclusive (i.e., items 13, 14, 15). Also, some information may be incorporated by reference to another statement being filed with the SEC and need not be duplicated in the S-1 filing.

Form S-1

Part I

1. Distribution Spread
2. Plan of Distribution
3. Use of Proceeds
4. Sales Otherwise than for Cash
5. Capital Structure
6. Summary of Earnings
7. Organization of Registrant
8. Parents of Registrant
9. Description of Business
10. Description of Property
11. Organization Within Five Years
12. Legal Proceedings
13. Capital Stocks Being Registered
14. Long-Term Debt Being Registered
15. Other Securities Being Registered
16. Directors and Executive Officers
17. Management Remuneration and Transactions

18. Securities Ownership of Certain Beneficial Owners and Management
19. Financial Statements
20. Brokerage Allocation

Part II

21. Marketing Arrangements
22. Other Expenses of Issuance and Distribution
23. Relationship with Registrants of Experts Named in Statement
24. Sales to Special Parties
25. Recent Sales of Unregistered Securities
26. Subsidiaries of Registrant
27. Franchises and Concessions
28. Indemnification of Directors and Officers
29. Treatment of Proceeds from Stock Being Registered
30. Financial Statements and Exhibits

A copy of a complete registration statement would be needed to explain the entire Form S-1. However, an examination of several items will appropriately illustrate the narrative and tabular nature of the form.

Using an S-1 filing for Valtek Incorporated, the front page and items 1,3,5,6,9,13, and 19 are shown in Exhibits 4-2 through 4-11. Even for these selected items, only a portion of the total is provided. A typical example of the cover page for an S-1 is presented as Exhibit 4-2 on page 73.

Item 1 (Distribution Spread) is intended to give a quick look at the distribution, price, and proceeds of the offering, and must appear on the cover page of the prospectus, as shown for Valtek Incorporated in Exhibit 4-3, page 74.

EXHIBIT 4-2

As filed with the Securities and Exchange Commission on October 12, 1976

Registration No. 2-57018

SECURITIES AND EXCHANGE COMMISSION

Washington, D. C. 20549

AMENDMENT NO. 2

To

FORM S-1

REGISTRATION STATEMENT

Under

THE SECURITIES ACT OF 1933

Valtek Incorporated

(Exact name of registrant as specified in charter)

765 South 100 East

Provo, Utah 84601

(Address of principal executive offices)

Telephone No. (801) 373-1100

CHARLES L. BATES

President

Valtek Incorporated

765 South 100 East

Provo, Utah 84601

(Name and address of agent for service)

Copies to:

ARTHUR J. SEIFERT, ESQ.
Dawson, Nagel, Sherman & Howard
2900 First of Denver Plaza
Denver, Colorado 80202

RICHARD G. BROWN, ESQ.
Poelman, Fox, Edwards & Oswald
36 South State Street, Suite 2000
Salt Lake City, Utah 84111

Approximate date of commencement of proposed sale to public:

As soon as practicable after the effective date of the Registration Statement.

EXHIBIT 4-3

DISTRIBUTION SPREAD

	Price to Public	Underwriting Discounts and Commissions (1)	Proceeds to the Company (2)(3)
Per Share	$ 4.50	$ .41	$ 4.09
Total	$1,575,000	$143,500	$1,431,500

The requirement in item 3 (Use of Proceeds) provides an example of the frequent use of narrative to supplement numerical information. Exhibit 4-4 illustrates how Valtek Incorporated proposed to use the proceeds of the offering.

EXHIBIT 4-4

USE OF PROCEEDS AND CAPITAL EXPENDITURES

The net proceeds to the Company from the sale of the Common Stock offered hereby are estimated to be $1,363,647. The table below sets forth the anticipated application of the estimated net proceeds.

Application	Amount
Construct and equip a sales, repair and assembly facility in Deer Park, Texas	$ 350,000
Purchase of production equipment	300,000
Repayment of loans secured by production equipment	300,000
Repayment of bank debt	300,000
Repayment of demand notes	80,000
Working capital (1)	33,647
TOTAL	$1,363,647

(1) This amount may increase by up to $143,150 if the Underwriters exercise the overallotment option.

The amount added to working capital will be used to purchase raw materials inventory and for other general corporate purposes. Pending utilization, the estimated net proceeds may be invested in short-term interest-bearing obligations or temporarily used to reduce remaining amounts outstanding pursuant to the Company's line of bank credit.

The Company has entered into an agreement to purchase approximately 19 acres of land in Springville, Utah, and has also acquired an option to purchase an adjoining tract of approximately 16 acres. The Company intends to construct on the property a new plant facility containing approximately 130,000 square feet of office and manufacturing space at an estimated cost of $3,000,000. Preliminary design work has been completed and bids have been received on site preparation; completion of the facility is estimated during the summer of 1977. Based on discussions and expressions of interest to date, the Company believes there are several available alternatives for financing of construction, including borrowing, leasing, or industrial revenue bonds. The Company is presently reviewing the various financing alternatives with a view to selecting the most economical method, but has made no arrangements for financing at the present time. See "Properties."

The capitalization table required by item 5 shows the company's debt and equity position just prior to the offering and on an "as if" basis reflecting the expected sale of securities. The following exhibit provides an example.

EXHIBIT 4-5

CAPITALIZATION

The following table sets forth the capitalization of the Company at July 31, 1976 and as adjusted to reflect the sale of shares offered hereby and the application of the estimated net proceeds of this offering.

Title of Class	Amount Outstanding at July 31, 1976	As Adjusted
Short-term debt:		
10% demand notes payable	$ 80,000	$ —0—
Current installments of long-term debt	72,502	17,342
	$ 152,502	$ 17,342
Long-term debt: (a)		
Note payable to bank	$ 950,000	$ 650,000
9¾% notes payable on buildings	561,326	561,326
9¾% note payable on equipment	243,253	—0—
Contracts payable on equipment	16,946	—0—
	1,771,525	1,211,326
Stockholders' equity:		
Common stock of $.20 par value Authorized 5,000,000 shares; outstanding 1,761,820 at July 31, 1976 and 2,111,820 to be outstanding (b)	352,364	422,364
Additional paid-in capital (c)	558,232	1,851,879
Retained earnings	1,096,925	1,096,925
Total stockholders' equity	2,007,521	3,371,168
Total capitalization	$3,779,046	$4,582,494

(a) See notes 4 and 9(a) to financial statements included elsewhere in this Prospectus for further information regarding long-term debt and long-term leases, respectively.

(b) Does not include 73,300 shares reserved for issuance upon exercise of outstanding stock options, nor up to 35,000 shares which may be sold to the Underwriters to cover overallotments. See "Stock Options" and "Underwriting."

(c) Net of stock issuance expense.

The requirement for item 6, the Summary of Earnings, is often met by including complete consolidated income statements, thus satisfying part of the requirements of item 19 at the same time. To meet both requirements, five years of certified income statements must be presented (refer to Exhibit 4-1), as is shown in Exhibit 4-6 on pages 76 and 77 for Valtek Incorporated.

EXHIBIT 4-6

VALTEK INCORPORATED
STATEMENTS OF EARNINGS

The following Statements of Earnings have been examined by Peat, Marwick, Mitchell & Co., independent certified public accountants, whose report with respect thereto appears elsewhere in this Prospectus and is qualified as to the consistency of application of generally accepted accounting principles as a result of the change in the method of valuing inventories as further explained in note 2 to the financial statements included elsewhere in this Prospectus. These statements should be read in conjunction with their separate notes and with the other financial statements and their related notes which are included elsewhere in this Prospectus.

	Years Ended April 30,				
	1972	1973	1974	1975	1976
Net sales	$1,382,344	2,032,967	2,611,582	4,655,187	7,162,595
Cost of sales (A)	872,429	1,229,248	1,504,913	2,707,235	3,835,460
Gross profit	509,915	803,719	1,106,669	1,947,952	3,327,135
Selling, general and administrative expenses:					
Commissions	204,402	311,904	420,412	814,280	1,238,229
Other selling expenses	140,207	157,155	229,648	337,985	491,003
General and administrative expenses	97,903	118,219	134,613	204,798	325,353
	442,512	587,278	784,673	1,357,063	2,054,585
Operating income	67,403	216,441	321,996	590,889	1,272,550
Other income (expense):					
Equity in loss by and other income from Canadian affiliate	—	(12,866)	(22,058)	(5,630)	12,631
Royalties from Canadian affiliate	—	1,520	15,327	31,285	52,181
Royalties from others	8,941	6,994	10,922	25,657	64,669
Disclosure fees	10,000	10,000	—	—	—
Miscellaneous	3,469	(1,847)	1,343	2,270	(6,878)
	22,410	3,801	5,534	53,582	122,603
Interest expense:					
Long-term	24,482	22,327	34,092	114,997	167,137
Short-term	21,878	18,056	23,661	22,128	27,209
	46,360	40,383	57,753	137,125	194,346
Earnings before income taxes	43,453	179,859	269,777	507,346	1,200,807
Income taxes (B)	17,211	78,015	120,480	227,000	560,000
Earnings before extraordinary item	26,242	101,844	149,297	280,346	640,807
Extraordinary item—Federal income tax benefit from loss carryover	20,300	—	—	—	—
Net earnings	$ 46,542	101,844	149,297	280,346	640,807
Primary and fully diluted earnings per share (C):					
Earnings before extraordinary item	$ .02	.06	.09	.16	.36
Extraordinary item	.01	—	—	—	—
Earnings per share	$ .03	.06	.09	.16	.36
Total shares used in computation of earnings per share (C)	1,575,220	1,611,886	1,670,658	1,751,360	1,771,651
Pro forma earnings per share (unaudited) (C)					$.35

See accompanying notes to the Statements of Earnings and notes to financial statements.

EXHIBIT 4-6 Continued

VALTEK INCORPORATED

NOTES TO STATEMENTS OF EARNINGS

(A)   In 1975, the Company changed its inventory valuation method to cost applied on the last-in, first-out (LIFO) method as further explained in note 2 to the financial statements included elsewhere in this Prospectus.

(B)   For information regarding total income tax expense see note 8 to financial statements included elsewhere in this Prospectus.

(C)   Earnings per share have been computed based on the weighted average number of shares outstanding during the period (as shown below) after giving effect to the assumption that all dilutive stock options and warrants were exercised at the beginning of the period with the proceeds therefrom being used to acquire treasury shares.

	1972	1973	1974	1975	1976
Weighted average shares	1,424,920	1,482,741	1,572,124	1,705,662	1,723,603
Effect of:					
Options	144,100	126,485	94,958	35,153	33,990
Warrants	6,200	2,660	3,576	10,545	14,058
Total shares used in computation	1,575,220	1,611,886	1,670,658	1,751,360	1,771,651

Pro forma earnings per share (unaudited) have been computed for 1976 (as shown below) after giving effect to the assumption that $880,000 from the proposed sale of stock had been used to reduce notes payable and long-term debt and had occurred as of May 1, 1975.

Total shares used in earnings per share computation above	1,771,651
Shares assumed issued for reduction of debt	176,000
Total shares used in computation of pro forma earnings per share	1,947,651
Net earnings	$ 640,807
Pro forma effect of reduced interest cost, net of $44,776 of additional income tax expense	42,814
Pro forma net earnings	$ 683,621

(D)   During 1976, the Company reduced the depreciable lives of small equipment from two years to one year. The effect of this change was to increase 1976 depreciation expense by $86,542 (decrease earnings per share by $.02). Total depreciation expense aggregated $50,341, $74,493, $89,882, $154,192 and $309,224 for the five years 1972 through 1976 respectively.

(E)   The following expenses were charged to cost of sales, selling and general and administrative expenses during the five years ended April 30, 1976.

	1972	1973	1974	1975	1976
Payroll taxes	$ 23,085	35,560	55,480	81,293	111,250
Research and development	47,648	66,810	94,136	157,874	201,624
Pension expense	—	1,495	15,727	28,916	110,048

Previously reported research and development costs for the four years ended April 1975, have been restated in the preceding table to include all engineering department costs, consistent with the 1976 presentation.

Pension expense increased in 1976 due to an increased number of employees who became eligible and certain changes made in the pension plan to meet requirements of the Employees Retirement Income Security Act.

(F)   No dividends were declared during the five years ended April 30, 1976.

The major portion of any registration statement is a written explanation of the various items included. One of the most important explanations concerns item 9 (Description of Business). An evaluation is made of significant aspects of a company's operations. Valtek began this section with the description shown in Exhibit 4-7 below. Following this introduction, a comprehensive review of products, marketing, research and development, patents, competition, government regulation, and employees was given. Thus a potential investor has an opportunity to evaluate numerous facets of the company's business.

EXHIBIT 4-7

THE COMPANY

Valtek Incorporated designs, develops, manufactures and markets automatic control valves and valve actuators. The valves are used primarily in industries requiring automatic control of the flow of liquids and gases. During the past three years the markets for the Company's products, in descending order of importance, and the approximate percentage of the Company's sales in such markets were as follows: chemical (45%); power (27%); industrial gases (11%); petroleum, metals and textiles (4% each); aerospace and food and drug (2% each); and paper (1%). Sales to ultimate users are made directly or through engineering contractors primarily by independent sales representatives located in principal market areas throughout the United States. The Company has also licensed three foreign companies, in Canada, England and Australia, to manufacture and market the Company's existing products. The licensees in England and Australia are unaffiliated with the Company. The Canadian licensee, Valtek Controls, Ltd., is a 34.7% owned affiliate of the Company.

The Company was incorporated under the laws of the State of Delaware in 1966, and was reincorporated under the laws of the State of Utah in 1968. The Company's executive offices are located at 765 South 100 East, Provo, Utah 84601, telephone (801) 373-1100. References to the "Company" or "Valtek" herein refer to Valtek Incorporated, unless the context requires otherwise.

Most investors are interested in the kind of security being offered and want to know the privileges and limitations inherent in the investment. Items 13, 14, and 15, depending on the type of security being registered, give an explanation of the rights and obligations pertaining to the security. Since Valtek's issue was common stock, the information in Exhibit 4-8 on page 79 appeared as a description.

Exposure to the narrative sections has been given to illustrate the wide variety of subjects covered. The financial statements included in Form S-1 have already been introduced by Exhibit 4-1. Valtek again provides a typical format. Appropriately accompanied by footnotes, the financial statements presented by Valtek include a Balance Sheet (Exhibit 4-9 on pages 80 and 81), Statements of Stockholders' Equity (Exhibit

EXHIBIT 4-8

DESCRIPTION OF COMMON STOCK

The Company is authorized to issue 5,000,000 shares of its Common Stock, $.20 par value, and as of April 30, 1976, 1,759,820 shares were issued and outstanding. Each holder of Common Stock is entitled to one vote for each share held on all matters voted upon by shareholders, including election of directors. The holders of Common Stock do not have cumulative voting rights or pre-emptive or other subscription rights to additional shares of the Company. Shares of Common Stock are not subject to redemption, calls or assessments, and outstanding shares of Common Stock are fully paid and non-assessable. The shares being sold by the Company pursuant to this Prospectus will, upon payment therefor, be fully paid and non-assessable.

The holders of Common Stock are entitled to receive dividends from funds legally available therefor, when and if declared, on such conditions and at such times as the Board of Directors may designate. In the event of any liquidation, dissolution or winding up of the Company, the holders of the Common Stock are entitled to receive a pro rata share of any assets distributable. The Common Stock does not have any conversion or redemption rights.

The Company furnishes annual reports to shareholders containing audited financial statements and quarterly reports containing unaudited financial information.

Atlas Stock Transfer, Inc., Salt Lake City, Utah, is the transfer agent for the Company's Common Stock.

4-10 on page 82), and Statements of Changes in Financial Position (Exhibit 4-11 on page 83).

As indicated earlier, Valtek followed common practice in furnishing five years of income statements to satisfy the summary of earnings requirement (item 6, shown as Exhibit 4-6) and at the same time meeting the requirements of item 19 with respect to income statements.[7]

Part II of Form S-1 requires additional backup information (see the listing on page 72) including appropriate signatures and consents of experts involved in the registration statements. These items are shown as Exhibits 4-12 and 4-13 respectively, on pages 84 and 85.

The process of review and acceptance of a registration statement has already been explained. The reader should now begin to understand why such a lengthy process is involved in the preparation and review of a registration statement. The other forms used for registration under the 1933 Act require additional specialized information as circumstances of the registrant change, but the basic disclosure of a company's business and financial position is common to all forms.

---

[7] Again recognize that this and other examples in Chapter 4 were prepared according to the existing requirements at the time of publication. Content changes will likely occur, but the general approach is illustrative.

EXHIBIT 4-9

VALTEK INCORPORATED

BALANCE SHEET

April 30, 1976

Assets

Current Assets:

Cash (note 4) .... $ 112,399

Receivables:

Trade accounts (net of allowance of $1,000) (note 4) 1,595,916

Canadian affiliate 154,508

Other 20,372

Total receivables 1,770,796

Inventories (notes 2 and 4) 1,695,927

Prepaid expenses 35,197

Total current assets 3,614,319

Investment in Canadian affiliate (note 11):

Equity .... (18,062)

Excess of cost over equity 14,484

Non-current advances 180,000

Total investment in Canadian affiliate 176,422

Cash surrender value of life insurance
(net of loans of $30,428) 6,977

Property, plant and equipment (notes 3 and 4) 2,035,687

Less accumulated depreciation .... (535,190)

Net property, plant and equipment 1,500,497

Deferred income tax charge 29,800

Patents, net of amortization 10,248

$5,338,263

See accompanying notes to financial statements.

EXHIBIT 4-9   Continued

VALTEK INCORPORATED
BALANCE SHEET
April 30, 1976

Liabilities and Stockholders' Equity

Current liabilities:

Current installments of long-term debt (note 4)	$ 70,941
10% Unsecured demand notes payable (note 4)	80,000
Accounts payable	348,581
Accrued expenses (note 5)	692,410
Income taxes payable (note 8)	407,226
Total current liabilities	1,599,158

Long-term debt excluding current
installments (note 4) 1,790,212

Stockholders' equity (note 7):

Common stock of $.20 par value Authorized 5,000,000 shares, issued 1,759,820 shares	351,964
Additional paid-in capital	601,233
Retained earnings	995,696
Total stockholders' equity	1,948,893

Commitments and contingent liabilities
(notes 6, 9, and 10)

$5,338,263

See accompanying notes to financial statements.

EXHIBIT 4-10

VALTEK INCORPORATED
STATEMENTS OF STOCKHOLDERS' EQUITY
Five Years Ended April 30, 1976

	1972	1973	1974	1975	1976
Common stock:					
Beginning of year	$ 275,234	287,234	310,344	328,774	342,224
Shares issued as a result of:					
Sale of 98,950 shares	—	19,790	—	—	—
Exercise of stock options of 60,000, 16,600, 92,150, 67,250 and 48,700 shares during 1972 through 1976, respectively	12,000	3,320	18,430	13,450	9,740
End of year	287,234	310,344	328,774	342,224	351,964
Additional paid-in capital:					
Beginning of year	251,955	270,050	450,564	510,253	537,585
Excess of proceeds over par value of comon stock issued as a result of:					
Sale of shares	—	128,635	—	—	—
Exercise of stock options	18,095	4,980	27,645	26,175	63,648
Income tax benefit resulting from sale of stock options by directors	—	46,899	32,044	1,157	—
End of year	270,050	450,564	510,253	537,585	601,233
Retained earnings (deficit):					
Beginning of year	(223,140)	(176,598)	(74,754)	74,543	354,889
Net earnings	46,542	101,844	149,297	280,346	640,807
End of year	(176,598)	(74,754)	74,543	354,889	995,696
Total stockholders' equity	$ 380,686	686,154	913,570	1,234,698	1,948,893

See accompanying notes to financial statements.

EXHIBIT 4-11

VALTEK INCORPORATED

STATEMENTS OF CHANGES IN FINANCIAL POSITION

Five Years Ended April 30, 1976

	1972	1973	1974	1975	1976
Sources of working capital:					
Net earnings before extraordinary item	$ 26,242	101,844	149,297	280,346	640,807
Items which do not use (provide) working capital:					
Depreciation and amortization	52,934	76,900	92,338	154,395	311,398
Equity in loss by Canadian affiliate	—	16,141	31,016	22,890	23,909
Deferred income taxes	(10,651)	11,016	11,580	56,500	20,400
Working capital provided by operations exclusive of extraordinary item	68,525	205,901	284,231	514,131	996,514
Extraordinary item—Federal income tax benefit derived from loss carryforward	20,300	—	—	—	—
Working capital provided by operations and extraordinary item	88,825	205,901	284,231	514,131	996,514
Proceeds from long-term borrowings	155,975	128,165	1,115,060	796,310	398,410
Proceeds from issuance of common stock	30,095	156,725	46,075	39,625	73,388
Proceeds from loans on life insurance	6,034	5,615	4,848	4,984	12,724
Deferred costs transferred to investment in Canadian affiliate	—	56,635	—	—	—
Proceeds from sale of equipment	—	1,842	1,525	26,477	2,826
Income tax benefits resulting from sale of stock options by directors	—	46,899	32,044	1,157	—
	$ 280,929	601,782	1,483,783	1,382,684	1,483,862
Uses of working capital:					
Additions to property, plant and equipment	$ 116,262	209,079	593,421	401,632	570,844
Current installments and repayment of long-term debt	44,885	62,671	612,756	312,491	73,024
Increase in cash surrender value of life insurance	8,474	1,596	5,012	12,658	10,748
Additions to patents	36	810	905	5,220	2,812
Non-current advances to Canadian affiliate	—	—	—	80,000	100,000
Investment in Canadian affiliate	—	64,297	—	27,690	—
Increase in working capital	111,272	263,329	271,689	542,993	726,434
	$ 280,929	601,782	1,483,783	1,382,684	1,483,862
Changes in components of working capital:					
Increase (decrease) in current assets:					
Cash	$ 3,183	8,134	22,682	4,196	65,513
Receivables	48,794	212,366	43,541	582,310	659,909
Inventories	50,587	141,788	405,721	483,144	367,634
Prepaid expenses	6,973	65	2,036	8,765	10,013
Deferred income tax charge	—	11,257	14,181	(20,892)	—
	109,537	373,610	488,161	1,057,523	1,103,069
Increase (decrease) in current liabilities:					
Current installments of long-term debt	(122,441)	3,686	(16,372)	16,117	10,831
Notes payable	—	—	—	160,300	(80,300)
Accounts payable	77,422	47,363	105,111	122,210	(154,258)
Accrued expenses	43,742	33,919	68,572	222,541	270,264
Income taxes payable	(458)	25,313	59,161	(6,638)	330,098
	(1,735)	110,281	216,472	514,530	376,635
Increase in working capital	$ 111,272	263,329	271,689	542,993	726,434

See accompanying notes to financial statements.

EXHIBIT 4-12

SIGNATURES

Pursuant to the requirements of the Securities Act of 1933, the Registrant has duly caused this Amendment No. 2 to the Registration Statement to be signed on its behalf by the undersigned, thereunto duly authorized, in the City of Salt Lake, State of Utah, on the 6th day of October, 1976.

VALTEK INCORPORATED

CHARLES L. BATES

By ....

Charles L. Bates, President

Pursuant to the requirements of the Securities Act of 1933, this Amendment No. 2 to the Registration Statement has been signed below by the following persons in the capacities and on the date indicated.

Signature	Title	Date

(1) PRINCIPAL EXECUTIVE OFFICERS:

Signature	Title	Date
CHARLES L. BATES Charles L. Bates	President and Director	October 6, 1976
LAWRENCE A. HAINES Lawrence A. Haines	Executive Vice President, Secretary and Director	October 6, 1976
FOREST E. ANTHONY Forest E. Anthony	Vice President, Assistant Secretary and Director	October 6, 1976

(2) PRINCIPAL FINANCIAL AND ACCOUNTING OFFICER:

Signature	Title	Date
DAVID R. ANDERSON David R. Anderson	Vice President—Finance	October 6, 1976

(3) DIRECTORS:

Signature	Title	Date
WILLIAM G. DIXON William G. Dixon	Director	October 6, 1976
DAVID B. HAIGHT David B. Haight	Director	October 4, 1976
HAL E. HOLMSTEAD Hal E. Holmstead	Director	October 6, 1976
HOWARD C. MAYCOCK Howard C. Maycock	Director	October 6, 1976

EXHIBIT 4-13

ATTORNEYS' CONSENT

The Board of Directors
Valtek Incorporated

We consent to the reference to our firm under the heading "Litigation" in the Prospectus as counsel for Valtek Incorporated.

POELMAN, FOX, EDWARDS & OSWALD

By: Richard G. Brown

Salt Lake City, Utah
October 4, 1976

ACCOUNTANTS' CONSENT AND REPORT ON SCHEDULES

The Board of Directors
Valtek Incorporated

The examination referred to in our report dated June 18, 1976 included the related supporting schedules for the three years ended April 30, 1976. In our opinion, such schedules present fairly the information set forth therein.

We consent to the use of our reports included herein and to the references to our firm under the headings "Statements of Earnings" and "Experts" in the prospectus.

PEAT, MARWICK, MITCHELL & CO.

Salt Lake City, Utah
October 4, 1976

Registration and Reporting Under the 1934 Act

Registration under the 1934 Act is a two-fold process. Before a security can be traded in the secondary markets, a registration statement must be on file with both the SEC and the exchange on which the security is to be traded. This requirement holds true even if a registration was made under the 1933 Act. Besides the dual registration, annual and other periodic reports are necessary. These provide a current record of all companies whose securities are traded. When securities are traded on over-the-counter markets, a registration with the SEC is also required—except for small companies—and the periodic reporting requirements must be met.

Registration requirements under the Securities Exchange Act of 1934 are almost identical to those of the Securities Act of 1933, so a review of that process need not be given. However, when a company registers its securities with an exchange, some added information is given. Included in the registration with the New York Stock Exchange is a ten-year Summary of Earnings (as opposed to five years for the SEC) and a Balance Sheet for two years (one year for the SEC). Registration on the American Stock Exchange requires a five-year Summary of Earnings, three-year statements of Stockholders' Equity and Changes in Financial Position, and a Balance Sheet for only one year. Regional exchanges vary in registration requirements.

Chapter 3 gives the forms used for registration with the SEC, and these forms are substantially duplicated for registering with the exchanges. Of more particular concern are (1) a review of the reporting documents submitted annually and quarterly to the SEC and (2) a comparison of these reports with the annual and quarterly reports to stockholders. As noted earlier, information disclosed in future reports to shareholders is expected to parallel more closely the information in reports filed with the SEC.

Annual Reports. The most common SEC annual report form is Form 10-K. This report must be filed within 90 days of the end of a company's fiscal year. Form 10-K is used to update the information a company gives with the registration statement; hence, the format is very similar to that of an S-1. Compare the list of disclosure items for Form 10-K (page 87) to the list given for Form S-1.

As an example of typical reporting for item 1 on Form 10-K, Exhibit 4-14 on pages 88 to 91 presents the cover page and selected information from Valtek Incorporated's 10-K for the fiscal year ended April 30, 1978.

Form 10-K

Part I
1. Business
2. Summary of Earnings
3. Properties
4. Parents and Subsidiaries
5. Legal Proceedings
6. Increases and Decreases in Outstanding Securities and Indebtedness
7. Changes in Securities and Changes in Security for Registered Securities
8. Defaults upon Senior Securities
9. Approximate Number of Equity Security Holders
10. Submission of Matters to a Vote of Security Holders
11. Indemnification of Directors and Officers
12. Financial Statements and Exhibits

Part II
13. Principal Security Holders and Security Holdings of Management and Executive Officers
14. Directors of the Registrant
15. Management Remuneration and Transactions

Item 1 (Business) covers the same broad spectrum of company operations given in the S-1 and comprises the major part of the narrative in the 10-K. The annual report to stockholders does not generally present such a lengthy discussion, but it is designed to summarize for the investor the business of the firm. With the changes in requirements for annual reports, explanation of the business will become more detailed, but the description is still not likely to be as detailed as in the 10-K.

An important section of the 10-K is management's discussion and analysis of the summary of earnings required by item 2. Exhibit 4-15 on pages 92 and 93 shows the information provided by Valtek, which highlights the major changes in earnings components between 1977 and 1978.

In terms of financial statements (item 12), any differences that exist between the reports filed with the SEC and those sent to shareholders will be in (1) the extent of detail provided, (2) the number of years for which information is presented, and (3) certification requirements.

As was mentioned earlier, some information is incorporated by reference to other reports and is not required to be duplicated. For example, Valtek made the statements shown at the top of page 88 with respect to item 11 and items 13 through 15, respectively.[8]

---

[8] The item numbers have been changed to correspond to the current Form 10-K.

Item 11—Indemnification of Directors and Officers
The information required by this item is unchanged from that reported
in item 17 of the Company's Form 10, filed October 20, 1971, which by
this reference is incorporated herein.

*Items 13 through 15 are omitted from this report, inasmuch as the Company
will file a definitive proxy statement pursuant to Regulation 14A, which
involves the election of directors, not later than 120 days after the close of
the fiscal year.*

EXHIBIT 4-14

SECURITIES AND EXCHANGE COMMISSION

Washington, D.C. 20549

FORM 10-K

Annual Report Pursuant to Section 13 or 15(d)
of the Securities Exchange Act of 1934

For the fiscal year ended April 30, 1978

Commission File No. 0-5862

VALTEK INCORPORATED

Utah	87-0272624
(State of Incorporation)	(IRS Employer Identification No.)

Mountain Springs Parkway
Springville, Utah 84663

Telephone: (801) 489-8611

Securities Registered Pursuant to Section 12(g) of the Act:

Common Capital Stock

Options to Purchase Common Capital Stock

Indicate by check mark whether the Registrant (1) has filed all
reports required to be filed by Section 13 or 15(d) of the Securities Exchange Act of 1934 during the preceding 12 months, and (2)
has been subject to such filing requirements for the past 90 days.

(1) Yes X___   No ___

(2) Yes X___   No ___

Class	Outstanding at April 30, 1978
Common stock, $.20 par value	2,137,690

EXHIBIT 4-14   Continued

ITEM 1.   Business.

(a) Valtek Incorporated (hereinafter the "Company")
designs, develops, manufactures and markets automatic control
valves and valve actuators. The valves are used primarily in
industries requiring automatic control of the flow of liquids and
gases. The markets for the Company's products include the
chemical, power, industrial gas, petroleum, paper, metals, food,
drug, textile, and aerospace industries. Sales to ultimate users
are made directly or through engineering contractors primarily by
independent sales representatives located in principal market
areas throughout the United States. The Company has also licensed
four foreign companies in Canada, England, Australia and Japan to
manufacture and market the Company's existing products. The
licensees in England, Australia and Japan are unaffiliated with
the Company. The Canadian licensee (Valtek Controls, Ltd.) is an
80 percent owned subsidiary of the Company.

During the past five years, there have been no significant
changes in the Company's basic product line except expansion to
include larger valves and valves with higher pressure ratings.
Emphasis has been placed on modular design to permit the Company
to assemble a variety of valve configurations from a relatively
small number of interchangeable parts.

In addition to its basic product line, the Company has
developed a line of "quiet flow" control valves in response to a
growing demand for valves capable of reducing noise levels
associated with high-pressure gas or liquid flows. The Company's
"Dragon Tooth" valve is designed to permit gradual rather than
abrupt changes in pressures which reduces noise to an acceptable
level and also substantially reduces cavitation (pitting of
internal valve parts) often associated with substantial pressure
reductions in the flow of liquids. Reduction of cavitation
results in longer valve life.

The Company manufactures and sells valves and valve parts for
installation in nuclear power plants pursuant to a nuclear code
stamp which was secured in March of 1974 and renewed in October of
1977 for a three-year period, after the American Society of
Mechanical Engineers determined that the Company's controlled
manufacturing system and quality assurance programs, as
implemented, were within the ASME code guidelines.

(b) 1.   The Company experiences active competition in the
sale of its basic product line of control valves and valve
actuators. The two major competitors are the Fisher Controls
Company of Marshalltown, Iowa, and Masoneilan International of
Norwood, Massachusetts, each of which has been established for
more than 50 years and both together produce the majority of
control valves sold in the United States. There are several other
competitors, some of which are older, larger, have more sales,
financial resources and facilities than the Company. In the quiet
control valve market the Company's main competitors are Control
Components, Inc. of Irvine, California, and Fisher Controls
Company.

The primary competitive factors in the industry are
price, delivery time, and product design and performance.
Although industry sales are not accurately tabulated, management
estimates its present sales to represent approximately four
percent of the total market for control valves in the United
States.

EXHIBIT 4-14   Continued

2.   During the year ending April 30, 1978, sales to the chemical, power, industrial gas and petroleum industries accounted for the majority of the Company's total sales. Two of the Company's customers, General Electric Company and Aramco, accounted for 12.8% and 11.2%, respectively, of total sales. While the loss of business from these customers could have a material adverse effect on the Company's business, such an occurrence is not considered likely.

3.   The Company estimates that its consolidated backlog as of April 30, 1978 was approximately $8,019,000, as compared to a backlog of approximately $6,641,000 at April 30, 1977. There are no seasonal aspects to this backlog and it is contemplated that the Company will be able to fill all present backlog during fiscal 1978, except orders for valves totaling approximately $666,000 for nuclear power plants and $262,000 for other valves which are scheduled for delivery over a three-year period.

Of the Company's backlog at April 30, 1978, approximately $1,454,000 (18.1%) was attributable to orders from General Electric Company. Of this amount, approximately $788,000 is scheduled for delivery in the current year and the balance is scheduled for delivery over the next succeeding two-year period.

In accordance with usual industry practice, orders are cancellable by customers at any time. These circumstances make it impossible for the Company to give assurance as to the "firm" nature of its backlog. The Company's experience, however, has been that commitments have been cancelled very infrequently. If an order is cancelled, a cancellation fee is usually imposed in an amount necessary to recoup direct and indirect costs which may vary depending on the degree of completion of the order, the materials used, and whether or not the products may be readily used in filling other orders.

4.   The principal raw materials used in manufacturing the Company's control valves are valve body castings, iron, steel, special alloys, and bar stock. Valve manufacturers have from time to time experienced delays and shortages in obtaining supplies of body castings as demand for the castings has occasionally exceeded foundry capacity. The Company has attempted to avoid such shortages and delays by ordering castings from a number of suppliers and by ordering basic castings annually in advance. The Company is not dependent upon any single source of supply for any of its raw materials and considers its relationship with its suppliers to be very good. The Company does not anticipate any difficulty in continuing to obtain its raw materials.

5.   The Company holds the right to a patent, which expires in 1987, covering certain construction features contained in all valves made by the Company. It also has obtained two patents relating to the "Dragon Tooth" quiet control valves, one of which (covering principal construction features of the valve as presently manufactured) expires in 1993, and the other patent (covering additional aspects of the valve) will expire in 1994. The Company has filed applications for patents in eight foreign countries, all of which cover the subject matter of the U.S. patent applications on the "Dragon Tooth" quiet flow control valve, of which two have issued. While the Company regards the patent covering the construction features of its basic valve line and the applications for patents covering the "Dragon Tooth" quiet flow control valve to be of material value, it does not believe that its ability to manufacture and sell its products is in any substantial way dependent upon such patents or patent applications. The Company's quiet flow control valves are

EXHIBIT 4-14   Continued

presently the subject of trademark and patent infringement litigation concerning the Company's right to manufacture and market the valves and the use of the trademark "Dragon Tooth." See Item 5, Legal Proceedings.

6.   The Company maintains an engineering department consisting of 20 professional personnel and five technicians. Of these, 17 are engaged in engineering work related to product development and eight are engaged in research related to new product design.

During the fiscal years ended April 30, 1978 and 1977, expenditures for research and development were $374,403 and $304,411, respectively. All such expenditures are expensed as incurred. The Company at present has no customer-sponsored research and development.

7.   As of April 30, 1978, the Company employed a total of 223 persons of whom 139 were in production, 42 in sales and marketing, 28 in engineering, and 14 in administration and other functions.

8.   The business of this company is not subject to compliance with any environmental laws or regulations and is not affected thereby.

9.   The business of the Company is not seasonal in any material aspect.

(c) 1.   The Company is engaged in only one line of business--the manufacturing and marketing of valves and valve parts.

2.   The Company has four licensees, identified as follows: Automatic Accessories, PTY, Ltd., an Australian firm which has been marketing the Company's products since January, 1969; Amalgamated Power Engineering, Ltd., an English firm which has been manufacturing and marketing the Company's products since September, 1972; Valtek Controls, Ltd., a Canadian subsidiary which was licensed in August, 1972, and began manufacturing and marketing the Company's products in January, 1973; and Nihon Koso Industrial Co. Ltd., a Japanese firm licensed in September, 1977. The Company's English licensee has a marketing area which includes the United Kingdom, most of Continental Europe and part of Africa. The market area of the Australian licensee includes Australia, New Zealand, Malaysia and Indonesia. The market area for the Canadian licensee consists of Canada and the market area for the Japanese licensee is Japan and Korea.

Under the terms of its license agreements, the Company is entitled to receive a royalty from its licensees generally based upon five percent of the sales value of licensed products. Royalties due from licensees for the past fiscal year amounted to $73,243 (excluding Canada, which is now a subsidiary of the Company).

3.   During the 1978 fiscal year sales to destinations outside of the United States amounted to approximately $3.5 million. Of this amount approximately nine percent was represented by sales in Canada made through the Company's Canadian subsidiary, and approximately 11 percent was represented by sales to Aramco, in Saudi Arabia. The balance is represented by sales to various foreign destinations. The Company is not aware of any particular risks incident to operations in the areas where it has made foreign sales.

EXHIBIT 4-15

MANAGEMENT'S DISCUSSION AND
ANALYSIS OF THE SUMMARY OF EARNINGS

The following table indicates the percentage of net sales for items shown in the Summary of Earnings for the years ended April 30:

	1978	1977	1976
Net Sales	100.0%	100.0%	100.0%
Cost of sales	55.4	49.9	53.5
Selling, general and administrative expenses	24.8	29.5	28.7
Other income	1.0	.8	1.7
Interest expense	2.5	1.4	2.7
Minority expense	.4	--	--
Income taxes	6.8	9.1	7.9
Net Earnings	11.1%	10.9%	8.9%

1978 COMPARED TO 1977

Net Sales have increased $4.2 million (45%) as the Company has continued to take a greater share of the growing market for automatic control valves. Major factors accounting for the increase are: (1) approximately $1 million due to consolidation of the Company's Canadian subsidiary, previously an affiliate accounted for on the equity method; (2) improved customer acceptance of the Company and its products; (3) the success of Valtek's Dragon Tooth valves; and (4) continued product line expansion.

Cost of Sales increased $2.9 million (61%) over 1977. Major factors giving rise to the increase in relation to sales were: (1) consolidation of the Company's Canadian subsidiary; (2) inefficiencies in the fully utilized old plant, the actual move to the new headquarters plant, and the start-up required in the new facility; (3) expensing of all moving costs; (4) new repair business in Houston with higher first year cost of sales.

Selling, General and Administrative Expenses increased $602,871 but were significantly less in relation to sales. Commissions to sales representatives were reduced by $215,068 primarily due to establishing a direct sales office in Houston, Texas on May 1, 1977. Increased direct foreign sales and a changing product mix also helped reduce the commissions as a percent of sales. Other expenses generally increased with volume of sales with some benefit from economies of scale except legal costs were higher and bad debt expense was lower.

Other Income increased as a result of approximately $75,000 in start-up costs which were incurred in opening the Houston sales facility in 1977 for which there is no corresponding expense in

EXHIBIT 4-15   Continued

1978. This increase has been partially offset by the effect of consolidating the Canadian subsidiary in 1978.

Interest Expense increased mainly due to increased borrowing to finance new plant and equipment and the effect of consolidating Canadian interest expense.

Minority Interest resulted from the additional purchase by the Company of Valtek Controls Ltd. stock and the subsequent consolidation (see note 15 to the financial statements).

Income Taxes (as a percentage of earnings before income taxes) was 38.0% for 1978 and 45.6% for 1977. The decrease in the effective tax rate was primarily due to the amount of investment tax credits and new jobs credit available to the Company and the effect of consolidating the Canadian subsidiary's earnings.

1977 COMPARED TO 1976

Net Sales increased $2.3 million (32%) as the Company took a greater share of the growing market for automatic control valves. Major factors accounting for the increases are: (1) improved customer acceptance of the maturing Company and its products; (2) expansion of product lines; (3) success of Valtek's new Dragon Tooth valves; and (4) sales to the nuclear power industry.

Cost of Sales increased $874,000; however, the overall efficiency of the manufacturing operation has improved with a reduction in cost of sales as a percentage of sales. Better use of facilities, increased automation, and improved manufacturing methods were principal factors in the reduction.

Selling, General and Administrative Expenses increased $740,000. The largest item in this category is commissions paid to sales representatives which increased $327,000. The relationship of commissions to sales varies from year to year, depending on market conditions and product mix. Other increases are basically volume related; however, the increase in expenses (as a percentage of sales) is due mainly to higher bad debt expenses, increased sales exhibit and advertising expenses, and higher legal costs.

Other Income decreased mainly due to the expensing of $75,000 of start-up costs associated with the Houston facility. These increased costs have been partially offset by an increase in income from licensees.

Interest Expense decreased due to the Company's reduced borrowing after proceeds from the stock offering reduced outstanding debt.

Income Taxes as a percentage of earnings before income taxes was 45.6% in 1977 and 46.7% in 1976. The difference is primarily due to investment credit.

Quarterly Reports. To keep both investors and experts apprised of interim changes in a company's operations and financial position, quarterly reports are prepared for stockholders and the SEC. From time to time the Commission changes this form in order to make the 10-Q more useful to analysts and investors. Form 10-Q was revised by ASR No. 177 and by ASR No. 206. The financial data currently required parallels closely the disclosures required in annual reports to the SEC, except that the 10-Q contains only quarterly and year-to-date information as noted in Exhibit 4-1. Previously the 10-Q only called for summary information. Another important change is the addition of management's narrative analysis of the results of operations.

All quarterly data should be prepared in accordance with generally accepted accounting principles as specified by the FASB and other authoritative accounting bodies. APB Opinion No. 28 provides reporting guidelines on this topic, although the FASB is currently reconsidering the provisions of that opinion. The Form 10-Q must be filed within 45 days after the end of each of the registrants' first three quarters. The information to be enclosed is listed below. An example of a 10-Q is provided in Exhibit 4-16 on pages 95 through 99.

Part I - Financial Information

1. Persons for Whom the Financial Information Is to Be Given
2. Preparation of Financial Information
3. Delay in Filing Financial Information
4. Financial Statements
5. Management's Analysis of Quarterly Income Statements
6. Other Financial Information
7. Reviews by Independent Public Accountants
8. Filing of Other Statements in Certain Cases
9. Exhibits

Part II - Other Information

1. Legal Proceedings
2. Changes in Securities
3. Changes in Security for Registered Securities
4. Defaults upon Senior Securities
5. Increase in Amount Outstanding of Securities or Indebtedness
6. Decrease in Amount Outstanding of Securities or Indebtedness
7. Submission of Matters to a Vote of Security Holders
8. Other Materially Important Events
9. Exhibits and Reports on Form 8-K

EXHIBIT 4-16

SECURITIES AND EXCHANGE COMMISSION
500 North Capitol Street, Room 130
Washington, D.C.   20549

Form 10-Q

Quarterly Report Under Section 13 or 15(d)
of the Securities Exchange Act of 1934

For Quarter Ended January 31, 1979 - Commission file number 0-5862

VALTEK INCORPORATED

State of Incorporation - Utah   I.R.S. Employer Identification No. 87-0272624

Mountain Springs Parkway, Springville, UT   84663

Telephone 801-489-8611

Indicate by check mark whether the registrant (1) has filed all reports required
to be filed by Section 13 or 15(d) of the Securities Exchange Act of 1934 during
the preceding 12 months (or for such shorter period that the registrant was required to file such report), and (2) has been subject to such filing requirements
for the past 90 days. Yes ___X___ No _____

Class	Outstanding
Common stock $.20 par value	2,150,870

EXHIBIT 4-16 Continued

VALTEK INCORPORATED

Consolidated Balance Sheets
January 31, 1979 and 1978
(Unaudited)

Assets:

	1979	1978
Current Assets:		
Cash	$ 42,678	115,058
Receivables:		
Trade accounts	3,354,994	2,066,321
Other	97,020	42,672
Less allowance for doubtful accounts	(24,000)	(23,703)
Total receivables	3,428,014	2,085,290
Inventories	5,543,928	3,833,717
Prepaid expenses	99,279	131,828
Total current assets	9,113,899	6,165,893
Property, plant and equipment	8,724,450	7,159,127
Less accumulated depreciation	(1,104,848)	(763,107)
Net property, plant and equipment	7,619,602	6,396,020
Net property and plant held for resale	580,943	-
Other assets, net of amortization	124,289	151,412
	$17,438,733	12,713,325

See accompanying notes to consolidated condensed financial statements.

EXHIBIT 4-16   Continued

Liabilities and Stockholders' Equity:

	1979	1978
Current Liabilities:		
Current installments of long-term debt	$ 118,920	38,484
Notes payable	2,596,600	67,748
Accounts payable	1,927,733	1,571,631
Accrued expenses	998,406	974,515
Income taxes payable	216,755	310,513
Total current liabilities	5,858,414	2,962,891
Long-term debt excluding current installments	4,730,195	4,360,976
Deferred income taxes	377,200	19,200
Minority interest	32,740	–
Stockholders' equity:		
Common stock of $.20 par value		
Authorized 5,000,000 shares; issued		
2,150,870 shares for 1979 and 2,134,240		
for 1978	430,174	426,848
Additional paid-in capital	2,080,880	1,982,675
Retained earnings	3,929,130	2,960,735
Total stockholders' equity	6,440,184	5,370,258
	$17,438,733	12,713,325

EXHIBIT 4-16   Continued

VALTEK INCORPORATED

Consolidated Summary of Earnings
Nine Months Ended January 31, 1979
(Unaudited)

	Three Months Ended January 31,		Nine Months Ended January 31,	
	1979	1978	1979	1978
Net sales	$4,395,890	3,374,026	9,953,223	8,442,120
Cost of sales	2,290,764	1,708,965	5,408,963	4,291,786
Gross profit	2,105,126	1,665,061	4,544,260	4,150,334
Selling, general and administrative expenses	1,293,099	924,276	3,536,341	2,399,381
Operating income	812,027	740,785	1,007,919	1,750,953
Other income	50,815	30,880	128,481	139,021
Interest expense	190,516	110,079	509,672	217,255
Minority interest	(6,966)	–	(2,100)	–
Earnings before income taxes	679,292	661,586	628,828	1,672,719
Income taxes	265,000	275,000	245,000	734,000
Net earnings	$ 414,292	386,586	383,828	938,719
Primary and fully diluted earnings per share	$ .19	.18	.18	.43
Dividends	None	None	None	None

See accompanying notes to consolidated condensed financial statements.

EXHIBIT 4-16   Continued

VALTEK INCORPORATED

Consolidated Condensed Statements of Changes in Financial Position
Nine Months Ended January 31, 1979 and 1978
(Unaudited)

	Nine Months Ended January 31, 1979	Nine Months Ended January 31, 1978
Sources of working capital:		
Working capital provided by operations	$ 772,502	1,157,214
Increase in long-term debt	533,372	3,800,000
Proceeds from issuance of common stock	44,172	17,676
Net effect of Canadian Consolidation	–	197,775
Other sources	32,500	–
Decrease in working capital	258,537	22,165
	$1,641,083	5,194,830
Uses of working capital:		
Additions to property, plant and equipment	$1,487,444	3,493,628
Current installments and repayment of long-term debt	135,877	1,580,458
Purchase of 78,053 shares of Valtek Controls Ltd.	–	78,053
Increase in other assets	17,762	42,691
	$1,641,083	5,194,830

See accompanying notes to consolidated condensed financial statements.

Generally stockholders do not receive the 10-Q. Instead, interim reports are sent to the stockholders. In comparative form, with brief explanations of a company's continuing operations, these reports present a short summary of sales and income.

Quarterly reports are submitted following the first three quarters of a company's reporting year. The annual reports then consolidate the year's operations. During the year, however, significant changes may take place in either a firm's policies or its financial position; and such changes are reported in the 10-Q or quarterly report. To ensure adequate disclosure of any such material event, Form 8-K, the so-called "current report," must generally be submitted to the SEC within 15 days after the occurrence of a significant event. The following list is representative of the items to be reported by Form 8-K:

1. A change in control of the registrant
2. Acquisition or disposition of a majority-owned subsidiary
3. The filing or termination of material legal proceedings
4. A material default on senior security
5. An increase or decrease of more than five percent in any class of outstanding security
6. A write-down, write-off, or abandonment of assets
7. Changes in the registrant's certifying accountants

Any other event of material importance must also be reported.

As with all other SEC forms, the 8-K has no specific format but is a narrative report of sufficient flexibility to permit management to describe any changes that may affect the firm. Financial statements accompany Form 8-K only when the form is submitted pursuant to an acquisition, and then only when the acquired company represents more than 15 percent of the total assets or revenues of the registering company.

Summary

Chapter 3 introduced the reader to the various forms and their uses. Chapter 4, while not analyzing all of the forms, has looked at those most commonly used for SEC registration and reporting and has compared them with the annual reports given to stockholders.

Over the past several years, disclosure to stockholders has been upgraded significantly. Much of the improvement has come as a result of SEC prompting, but managements have also responded on their own initiative to provide stockholders with more adequate information. The comparisons made in this chapter illustrate some similarities and differences among reports to stockholders and reports to the SEC. Though the detail may seem tedious, the result is that the average American investor has never been more adequately supplied with information concerning companies in which investments are made.

Chapter 5 will focus attention on the interaction between the SEC and the business community, particularly the accounting profession.

DISCUSSION QUESTIONS

1. How many different annual reports do managements prepare? To whom do these reports go?

2. Have there been any significant changes in the disclosure in annual reports to stockholders during the past 40 years? What are they?

3. What are some of the more important disclosure requirements for annual reports?

4. What are the most common forms sent to the SEC? What information do they contain?

5. What are some of the major differences between the registration reports filed with the SEC and with an exchange?

6. What is the nature of Form 8-K?

7. In what ways will financial statements sent to the SEC be different from financial statements sent to shareholders?

CHAPTER 5

IMPACT OF THE SEC ON THE ACCOUNTING PROFESSION AND THE BUSINESS COMMUNITY

Two of the most interesting and important topics concerning the SEC are the role the Commission plays in the development of accounting principles and the impact the SEC has had and will continue to have on the accounting profession and business in general. The variety of responsibilities discussed in earlier chapters pursuant to the SEC's broad statutory powers makes the Commission an important partner in the business community.

In this chapter, the SEC's accounting-related authority is examined. A discussion of accounting practices and problems arising as a result of this legal authority is also presented. Finally, an examination of the interaction of the SEC with the accounting profession in developing accounting principles and auditing standards places this important topic in perspective.

SEC Authority Relative to Accounting Practice

The SEC has the statutory authority to regulate and to prescribe the form, content, and compilation process of financial statements and other reports. This authority has led to a close and continued interaction between the SEC and the accounting profession in the development of financial accounting and reporting principles and practices as well as auditing standards and procedures. A recognition and appreciation of this interaction has been lacking among accounting students and professionals. Therefore, the reasons for the SEC's broad regulatory authority with respect to financial accounting and reporting practices are examined briefly.

Congressional Authority

Congress recognized that the SEC would need some control of accounting principles and procedures in order to fulfill its goal of full and fair disclosure. The regulatory authority given to the SEC was considerably influenced by the wide variation in accepted accounting principles and procedures evident in the late 1920s. Some observers felt that this variation may have contributed to the stock market crash and to the decline of the economy in general. In any event, Congress desired to provide adequate disclosure of information for investors and gave the SEC authority to prescribe the accounting principles and procedures to be used in the financial statements it receives.

Congressional Acts. The first Congressional grant of accounting authority was to the Federal Trade Commission in the Securities Act of 1933. Section 19(a) of the Act delineates this responsibility:

> . . . shall have authority . . . to prescribe the form or forms in which required information shall be set forth, the items or details to be shown in the balance sheet and earning statement, and the methods to be followed in the preparation of accounts, in the appraisal or valuation of assets and liabilities, in the determination of depreciation and depletion, in the differentiation of recurring and nonrecurring income, in the differentiation of investment and operating income, and in the preparation, where the Commission deems it necessary or desirable, of consolidated balance sheets or income statements. . . .

Thus, the 1933 Act gave the FTC, and subsequently the SEC, very broad powers to prescribe any forms, rules, procedures, and regulations it deemed necessary to fulfill its obligations under the law. Included is the authority to have the last word on any accounting matter related to companies filing under the Act.

With the 1934 Act and the formation of the SEC, the new Commission inherited the authority of the 1933 Act and received additional authority for companies filing periodic reports. Section 13(b) of the 1934 Act states:

> The Commission may prescribe, in regard to reports made pursuant to this title, the form or forms in which the required information shall be set forth, the items or details to be shown in the balance sheet and the earning statement, and the methods to be followed in the preparation of reports, in the appraisal or valuation of assets and liabilities. . . .

The section continues in a manner similar to the 1933 Act. Thus, the regulatory powers relative to accounting practice under the 1934 Act are substantially the same as those under the 1933 Act.

It should be noted that the SEC's authority extends only to companies that must file statements with it. However, due to the interaction between such standard-setting bodies as the American Institute of Certified Public Accountants, the Financial Accounting Standards Board (FASB), and the SEC in developing reporting standards, and due to the size and importance of the filing companies and their auditors, it is probably not an exaggeration to state that the SEC's regulatory power extends to virtually all public accounting situations. Furthermore, because of the provisions in the 1934 Act covering proxy statements, the SEC has been granted regulatory power with respect to the accounting procedures used in preparing annual reports to stockholders as well as reports to the SEC. Under this authority, the requirements for stockholders' reports were promulgated (see Chapter 4). The accounting provisions of the Foreign Corrupt Practices Act of 1977 give added authority under the 1934 Act and have the potential for greatly expanding prescribed accounting practice.

The Public Utility Holding Company Act of 1935 gives the Commission even broader authority over accounting practice than the 1933 or 1934 Acts. The SEC not only can specify the forms, procedures, and regulations to be used in filing forms with it, but also can specify the accounting system and its function within the registered companies. Section 10(a) contains the following:

> The Commission shall have authority from time to time to make, issue, amend, and rescind such rules and regulations and such orders as it may deem necessary or appropriate . . . including rules and regulations defining accounting, technical and trade terms used. . . . The Commission shall have authority to prescribe the form . . . in which any statement, declaration, application, report, or other document filed with the Commission shall be set forth, the items or details to be shown in balance sheets, profit and loss statements, and surplus accounts, the manner in which the cost of all assets, whenever determinable, shall be shown in regard to such statements, declarations, applications, reports, and other documents filed with the Commission, or accounts required to be kept by the rules, regulations, or orders of the Commission, and the methods to be followed in the keeping of accounts and cost accounting procedures and the preparation of reports, in the segregations and allocation of costs, in the determination of liabilities . . . depletion and depreciation . . . income . . . consolidated balance sheets or profit and loss statements for any companies in the same holding-company system.

The other Acts administered by the SEC give added authority in accounting procedures as they relate to investment companies and broker-dealers.

Other Congressional Considerations. Another factor which may have led Congress to give the SEC broad power to regulate accounting was the recognized dependence of the investor on the opinion of the accountant. This dependence is noted by Harry A. McDonald, a former Commissioner of the SEC. He said:

> One fact will always be dominant in shaping the course of accounting—the fact that whether directly or through his advisers, whether alone or through the medium of an agency like the SEC, the investor cannot help but look to the accountant.[1]

The idea of having government accountants do business auditing pervaded Congress for a while, but the idea was finally replaced. Instead, Congress recognized the importance of the independent public accountant and specified that financial statements filed with the SEC had to be certified by this independent agent.

SEC Authoritative Pronouncements

In exercising the broad regulatory authority described above, the SEC has relied primarily upon generally accepted accounting principles as established by the accounting profession. In fact, the SEC has explicitly stated in ASR No. 150 that it considers those accounting principles, standards, and practices promulgated by the FASB as having substantial authoritative support. The SEC thus recognizes the FASB as the primary standard-setting body in the private sector. However, pursuant to its legal authority, the SEC can and does issue several types of authoritative pronouncements which clarify, modify, amend, or even supersede accounting principles established by other bodies. The sources of information relative to SEC reporting were identified in Chapter 3. Four of the major SEC documents are described in the next few paragraphs.

Regulation S-X is the principal source relating to the form and content of financial statements to be included in registration statements and financial reports filed with the Commission, but it does not contain all of the SEC views on accounting principles. Regulation S-X, codified in 1940, is continually being revised. Any accountant involved in SEC registration and reporting must be familar with S-X and its requirements.

---

[1] Harry A. McDonald, "How Cooperation in Development of Accounting Principles by SEC and Profession Helps Investors," *Journal of Accountancy* (March, 1951), p. 415.

Louis H. Rappaport stresses that "no public accountant should attempt an examination of financial statements intended for filing under any of these Acts without having an up-to-date copy of Regulation S-X at hand."[2]

Regulation S-K, Integrated Disclosure Rules, is a set of instructions for regulation of business and properties. It is similar in intent to Regulation S-X. As indicated, S-X prescribes the form and content of financial statements for SEC filings; S-K prescribes the requirements for nonfinancial statement information for SEC reporting. S-K also covers certain aspects of annual reports to shareholders. As an example, disclosure of the results of operations of major business segments is not required by S-X in the financial statements but is required by S-K. Regulation S-K should make the additional nonfinancial statement disclosure requirements more consistent over the various SEC forms.

Accounting Series Releases (ASRs) are also important SEC pronouncements of special interest to accountants. These releases primarily explain accounting procedures needing special treatment. Being of such importance, they require special notice. ASRs also relate to disciplinary sanctions imposed by the Commission. The releases began in 1937 and there are now over 250 ASRs. Many of these releases, however, have been replaced by subsequent releases, modified, or rescinded.

Just as the Accounting Principles Board (APB) issued authoritative opinions and the Financial Accounting Standards Board and the Cost Accounting Standards Board (CASB) now issue standards, the SEC keeps abreast of changing requirements by issuing accounting guidelines as ASRs. A current file is a must for any accountant working with SEC-related reports.

In November, 1975, the SEC, through its division of Corporation Finance and Office of Chief Accountant, began issuing Staff Accounting Bulletins (SABs). The documents are not official rules or interpretations of the Commission; however, they represent interpretations and practices followed by the staff of the SEC in administering the disclosure requirements of the federal securities laws. Therefore, they are important documents for accountants and managements to be familiar with.

The involvement of the SEC in accounting practice has resulted in a considerable body of literature on accounting principles. It is also important to note that many of the SEC pronouncements carry the force of law, not just recommended adherence. Some examples are discussed below.

---

[2] Louis H. Rappaport, *SEC Accounting Practice and Procedure* (3d ed.; New York: Ronald Press Co., 1972), pp. 16.1-16.2.

SEC Impact on Accounting and Business Practice

There are many areas in accounting and business where the SEC has had a significant influence in the development of current practices. Obviously, not all such areas can be discussed. Specific illustrations presented in this chapter relate to (1) changes in auditing procedures, (2) increased legal liabilities for managers, accountants, attorneys, and others, (3) new financial disclosure requirements for businesses, and (4) regulation of the accounting profession.

Auditing Changes

Although it does not prescribe auditing standards and procedures, the SEC has had considerable influence over them. By reviewing specific cases, the SEC has highlighted problems and motivated the accounting profession to take the necessary steps to correct deficiencies by developing additional auditing standards and procedures. The following cases are illustrative.

The McKesson and Robbins Case. The *McKesson and Robbins* case shows how an initial SEC review led to subsequent action by the accounting profession and resulted in revised and updated auditing standards.[3] In this well-known case, several millions of dollars of fictitious receivables and inventories were certified by the auditors. The SEC found that the auditing procedures followed were not sufficient, even though they were in accord with the generally accepted auditing procedures at that time. The accounting profession took immediate action in establishing additional standards—the audit practices for confirmation of receivables and for observation of inventories. In view of the responsive action by the accounting profession, the SEC apparently decided to continue to allow the profession to develop auditing procedures, subject to its approval, as specified in ASR No. 73.

The Yale Express Case. Another example of SEC action leading to subsequent revision of auditing standards by the accounting profession is the now well-publicized *Yale Express* case.[4] In this case the SEC filed an *amicus curiae* brief stating that accountants have a duty to disclose subsequent discovery of material error existing at the report date in financial statements which were previously certified. This action led to

---

[3] *Dennis* v. *McKesson and Robbins, Inc.,* U.S.D.C. District of Columbia Civil Action No. 66 (1938).

[4] *Fischer* v. *Kletz,* 266 F. Supp. 181 S.D.N.Y. (1967).

the issuance of a Statement on Auditing Procedure (SAP No. 47) which detailed the procedures to be followed by auditors upon subsequent discovery of events affecting their opinions on financial statements previously certified.

Independence of Accountants. Another important area in which the SEC has helped develop standards, although in a different manner, is in defining the concept of independence. Although the accounting profession had long realized and required that an auditor must be independent, the SEC, through Regulation S-X, ASR No. 13 (which defines the form of the auditor's certificate), and ASR No. 22 (which defines independence), took the lead in insisting on the observance of strict rules in determining independence. The accounting profession subsequently incorporated the SEC requirements into its code of professional ethics. ASR No. 234 provides current guidance on the Commission's policies pertaining to the independence of accountants.

A recent example of the SEC's interest in the independence of accountants is the issuance of ASR No. 250. In this release, the SEC adopted rules concerning the disclosure of auditors' services in a company's proxy statement. The SEC will require companies to disclose the following:

1. The percentage of total nonaudit service fees to the total annual audit fee
2. Individual nonaudit services which have fees greater than three percent of the annual audit fee
3. All nonaudit services provided by the independent auditor
4. Whether the board of directors or its audit committee had approved the services provided, after considering if such services would impair the auditors' independence

The implication is that the independence of a public accountant who provides nonaudit services requires special scrutiny. The SEC seems to be suggesting that disclosure of services will help protect independence. Whether or not this is true, the rules on disclosure of services and fees are a part of the Commission's continuing effort to strengthen the independence of auditors.

Auditing Procedures. The influence of the SEC on official auditing statements is also apparent. Many of the AICPA's Statements on Auditing Procedure had their beginning as a result of particular cases heard before the SEC. This is not to say that the AICPA Committee on Auditing Procedure has not made an effective contribution. It may, however, suggest the difficulty in determining audit procedures for situations that have not yet occurred and in combating defalcations or other deceptive practices that have not yet happened.

Fraud Detection. A final illustration relative to SEC influence on auditing deals with the detection of fraud. Due to its limited number of staff people, the SEC has had to rely on professionals such as accountants, lawyers, and underwriters to assist in the discovery of misrepresentation or fraud. The independent public accountant, because of the thorough examination performed in the audit, is viewed as being in a strategic position to detect any defalcations that could substantially misrepresent the financial position of a firm. As distasteful as this situation is to most practitioners, the SEC seems to be using accountants to assist in its policing efforts.

The impetus for fraud detection seems to be the result of increased litigation generally. To prevent unwanted lawsuits, accountants are being forced to devise stricter audit procedures that have a better chance of detecting fraud at a client company. If accountants are required to concentrate more on fraud detection, future audits will have to be much more extensive and costly. Auditing will become even more elaborate, and managements must be prepared to foot the bill for the expanded review. Naturally, there is opposition to this movement toward greater fraud detection, as evidenced by the following quotation:

> The SEC's ideas are directly contrary to a bedrock auditing tenet—that a routine audit can't be relied on to turn up fraud, because such an audit is too limited and the auditor too dependent on figures provided by the client.
>
> A routine audit is designed mainly to make sure that all transactions reported by the company are treated in accord with good accounting practice . . . . Generally accepted auditing standards hold an auditor responsible for failing to uncover fraud only if his failure results from failing to follow generally accepted auditing standards.[5]

However, several large corporate frauds have come to light during the past ten years (e.g., the *Equity Funding* case), some of which have been perpetrated for several years. Accountants are having difficulty arguing that a massive swindle is beyond the scope of an audit conforming to generally accepted auditing standards.

On the other hand, a ruling of the U.S. Court of Appeals suggests that accountants are not automatically to be viewed as an enforcement arm of the SEC. In a unanimous decision, the federal court affirmed a

---

[5] Frederick Andrews, "SEC Jolting Auditors Into a Broader Role in Fraud Detection," *Wall Street Journal* (July 12, 1974), p. 1.

lower court's finding that a major accounting firm neither violated nor fostered violations of the securities laws by GeoTek Resources Fund, Inc., in their audit of GeoTek. Applicable excerpts of the ruling are of interest.

> The SEC in the trial court appears to have asserted that the auditors performed their work "with blinders on" and that they should have done "more" to reveal to investors the conduct of the promoter and his associates that increased the financial risks of those who invested in his ventures. During oral argument the SEC appeared to take the position that the proper standard is whether the accountant performed his audit functions in a manner that would have revealed to an ordinary prudent investor, who examined the accountant's audits or other financial statements, a reasonably accurate reflection of the financial risks such an investor presently bears or might bear in the future if he invested in the audited endeavor.

> To accept the SEC's position would go far toward making the accountant both an insurer of his client's honesty and an enforcement arm of the SEC. We can understand why the SEC wishes to so conscript accountants. Its frequently late arrival on the scene of fraud and violations of securities laws almost always suggests that had it been there earlier with the accountant it would have caught the scent of wrongdoing and, after an unrelenting hunt, bagged the game. What it cannot do, the thought goes, the accountant can and should. The difficulty with this is that Congress has not enacted the conscription bill that the SEC seeks to have us fashion and fix as an interpretive gloss on existing securities laws.[6]

Detailed rules for the detection of fraud have not been developed by the SEC. Instead, the Commission has taken a case-by-case approach to enforcement. Without definitive guidelines, the SEC seems to be indicating its expectation that the accounting profession should develop appropriate auditing standards with respect to fraud detection. The final resolution of the accountant's auditing role, especially in connection with fraud detection, is perhaps years away. Auditors must be aware, however, of the changing expectations and requirements so that proper adjustments may be made in the scope of the audit examination.

Legal Liability

The second area of discussion is that of professional legal liability. An accountant or other professional must be aware of the possibilities of

---

[6] *SEC v. Arthur Young & Co.*, 590 F. 2d 785 (1979).

legal action stemming from professional activities. In many cases, knowledge of possible legal consequences of certain actions may make the difference between a successful professional career and a lawsuit which could result in financial ruin and loss of professional reputation.

The increase in litigation during the past several years may be attributed to a variety of causes. First, managements and all professionals have been increasingly subjected to damage suits stemming from their alleged negligence in fulfilling responsibilities. Second, banks, other creditors, and investors have found in a number of cases that they have been able to recoup their losses from the managers or from the accountants who prepared and certified the financial statements of the entity. Lastly, there has been a general trend during the past ten years towards increasing legal action that attempts to hold companies and those associated with them, including accountants, liable to the consuming public.

Nature of Liability. To understand the implications of the accountant's legal liability under the Securities Acts, an examination of liability under the common law is necessary. The liability under the Securities Acts, an extension of common law liability, is a Congressional attempt to hold accountants and others involved in Securities Acts registrations more strictly liable to third parties than they would be under the common law. Recent cases have expanded the scope of liability under both the common law and the Securities Acts. Thus, an accountant's liability under the common law may be conveniently divided into two parts: (1) liability to clients and (2) liability to third parties.

Liability to Clients. An accountant is liable to clients for negligence in the performance of professional duties and for breach of confidence. Negligence, and not an error in judgment, must be proven and must have resulted in a loss for the client. The accountant must possess the skills reasonably expected of a professional, and must exercise due care during the professional engagement in order to avoid a charge of negligence by a client.[7]

Accountants, like other professionals, acquire a considerable amount of information about their clients. Such information may be harmful to the client if disclosed to the public and competitors, so the law recognizes that the accountant has a fiduciary duty not to disclose confidential information. Since the accountant is considered to have a duty to the public, the recent rise in consumerism has imposed tighter limits on

---

[7] "Legal Liability of Auditors," *Touche-Ross Tempo* (March, 1966), p. 7.

what is considered confidential information between the accountant and the client.

Liability to Third Parties. As the fiduciary duty to clients has been limited, liability to third parties and the public has been expanded. Originally, third parties were held to have very limited recovery rights due to the lack of a contractual relationship between the accountant and the third party. A landmark case in the development of liability to third parties was *Ultramares Corporation* v. *Touche*,[8] in which Judge Cardozo of the Court of Appeals ruled that the accountants owed no duty to third parties to perform their examinations without negligence. He said:

> Our holding does not emancipate accountants from the consequences of fraud. It does not relieve them if their audit has been so negligent as to justify a finding that they had no genuine belief in its adequacy, for this again is fraud. It does no more than say that, if less than this is proved, if there has been neither reckless misstatement nor insincere profession of an opinion, but only honest blunder, the ensuing liability for negligence is one that is bounded by the contract, and is to be enforced between the parties by whom the contract has been made. We doubt whether the average businessman receiving a certificate without paying for it, and receiving it merely as one among a multitude of possible investors, would look for anything more.

Judge Cardozo, therefore, set the precedent that accountants would not be liable for mere negligence but would be liable to third parties for fraud and gross negligence amounting to fraud. In subsequent cases the liability to third parties has been extended. It now seems accountants might be held liable to third parties for fraud, gross negligence amounting to fraud, and for ordinary negligence when the accountant knows that the work is being done primarily for the benefit of specified third parties.

Accountants may even be held liable to third parties for ordinary negligence, regardless of who benefits from the work performed. Such a conclusion was suggested as early as 1959 by Professor R. F. Salmonson. His basic reasoning was that as professionals, accountants will rightly be held strictly liable to all who rely on their statements and representations.[9]

The accountant's defense might be adherence to well-defined professional standards. Problems arise, however, when professional standards

---

8 225 N.Y. 170, 174 N.E. 441 (1931).
9 R. F. Salmonson, "CPA's Negligence, Third Parties and the Future," *Accounting Review*, Vol. 34 (January, 1959) p. 91.

are under constant review by various policy-making groups, e.g., the FASB, the AICPA, and the SEC. The auditor must stay abreast of any changes in auditing standards if liability is to be minimized.

Legal Precedents. The *1136 Tenants' Corporation* case adds another dimension to the auditor's liability to clients and third parties.[10] The lower courts ruled that auditors performing write-up work may be held liable for certain audit procedures even though they did not contract to do an audit. This attempt to increase accountants' legal responsibilities has had a pronounced effect on the profession. It suggests that accountants should very carefully stipulate in every engagement the responsibility assumed and what procedures will be followed.

The *Continental Vending* case is also significant for two reasons.[11] First, two accountants were held criminally liable even though they apparently did not benefit directly from the misstatements in the financial statements. Second, it was established by experts that the accountants followed generally accepted auditing procedures. The Court of Appeals ruled, however, that the mere following of these procedures may not be enough to hold an accountant guiltless. The accountant must also be sure that the statements certified are not on the whole misleading to the average prudent investor. In the future, following the profession's standards may not be enough. The accountant's work may be judged according to whether or not lay investors would consider the certified financial statements as providing adequate disclosure.

Provisions Under the 1933 Act. Liability under the Securities Acts makes even more explicit the need for accountants and managers to be cautious and thorough in financial presentations and audit examinations. Section 11(a) of the 1933 Act assigns liability for misleading registration statements to the following people:

> (1) every person who signed the registration statement; (2) every person who was a director of (or person performing similar functions) or partner in, the issuer . . . ; (3) every person who with his consent, is named . . . as being or about to become a director . . . ; (4) every accountant, engineer, or appraiser, or any person whose profession gives authority to a statement made by him, who has with his consent been named as having prepared or certified any part of the registration statement . . . (5) every underwriter . . .

The effect of this act on the accountant's liability has been sum-

---

[10] *1136 Tenants' Corporation* v. *Max Rothenberg & Company,* 319 N.Y.S. 2d 1007 (1970).
[11] *U.S.* v. *Simon, et. al.,* 425 F 2d 796 (1969).

marized as follows:

1. Any person acquiring securities described in the Registration Statement may sue the accountant, regardless of the fact that he is not the
   client of the accountant.
2. His claim may be based upon an alleged false statement or misleading omission in the financial statements, which constitutes his *prima
   facie* case. The plaintiff does not have the further burden of proving
   that the accountants were negligent or fraudulent in certifying to the
   financial statements involved.
3. The plaintiff does not have to prove that he relied upon the statement or that the loss which he suffered was the proximate result of
   the falsity or misleading character of the financial statement.
4. The accountant has thrust upon him the burden of establishing his
   freedom from negligence and fraud by proving that he had, after
   reasonable investigation, reasonable ground to believe and did believe that the financial statements to which he certified were true not
   only as of the date of the financial statements, but beyond that, as of
   the time when the Registration Statement became effective.
5. The accountant has the burden of establishing by way of defense or
   in reduction of alleged damages, that the loss of the plaintiff resulted
   in whole or part from causes other than the false statements or the
   misleading omissions in the financial statements. Under the common law it would have been the plaintiff's affirmative case to prove
   that the damages which he claims he sustained were proximately
   caused by the negligence or fraud of the accountant.[12]

Important points to note are that (1) the accountant may be liable for
ordinary negligence to any person acquiring the securities, and (2) the
accountant must prove (as opposed to the common law where the
plaintiff has the burden of proof) either that the plaintiff's loss resulted
from causes other than the misleading statements or that the accountant
had, after reasonable investigation, grounds to believe and did believe
that the financial statements were true as of the effective date.

The defense outlined under the 1933 Act is called the "due diligence"
defense. That is, the parties to the registration must show that they
exercised care in preparing and reviewing not only their part of the
forms but also the entire statement. The most important case in this area
is *Escott* v. *BarChris Construction Corporation*.[13]

In the *BarChris* case, the accountants were held liable for certifying
material errors in the financial statements and for conducting an inade-

---

[12] Saul Levy, *C.P.A. Handbook* (New York: American Institute of Certified Public Accountants, 1952), p. 39.
[13] 283 F. Supp. 643 S.D.N.Y. (1968).

quate review. The S-1 review, which is conducted from the date of the certified financial statements until approximately the effective date of the registration, is intended to uncover any information that may indicate that the certified financial statements contain material errors and to satisfy the accountant's due diligence requirement.

Stipulations of the 1934 Act. It was generally believed until a few years ago that the principal liability threat for the business community under the 1934 Act was Section 18. The applicable part reads as follows:

> Any person who shall make or cause to be made any statement in any application, report, or document filed pursuant to this title or any rule or regulation thereunder or any undertaking contained in a registration statement as provided in subsection (d) of section 15 of this title, which statement was at the time and in the light of the circumstances under which it was made false or misleading with respect to any material fact, shall be liable to any person (not knowing that such statement was false or misleading) who, in reliance upon such statement, shall have purchased or sold a security at a price which was affected by such statement, for damages caused by such reliance, unless the person sued shall prove that he acted in good faith and had no knowledge that such statement was false or misleading.

Under the 1934 Act, the accountant is generally liable only to the date of financial statements, not the effective date, as under the 1933 Act. Management, however, assumes liability for the financial statements as long as they are used by the third parties. Also, a plaintiff must prove (as opposed to the 1933 Act where the accountant/manager has the burden of proof) that personal reliance upon the financial statements was the actual cause of damages incurred. Finally, the accountant is apparently not liable to third parties for ordinary negligence since it must be shown only that the accountant acted in good faith and had no knowledge that the statements were misleading. Managements assume responsibility for ordinary negligence. This is equivalent to the common law liability to third parties.

In addition to Section 18, liability has been found under Section 10(b) of the 1934 Act. In the now famous case involving Yale Express Systems, Inc., a major accounting firm was held liable under Rule 10b-5, which states:

> It shall be unlawful for any person, directly or indirectly, by the use of any means . . .
> (a) to employ any device, scheme, or artifice to defraud,
> (b) to make any untrue statement of a material fact or to omit to state a material fact necessary in order to make the statements made, in the

light of the circumstances under which they were made, not misleading, or,
(c) to engage in any act, practice, or course of business which operates
or would operate as a fraud or deceit upon any person, in connection
with the purchase or sale of any security.

The accounting firm failed to disclose information which it obtained
in a management services engagement subsequent to an audit engagement. The information indicated that the financial statements which the
firm certified as a result of the audit contained false and misleading
statements. The court held that the accounting firm's silence amounted
to a device to omit a material fact necessary to make the statements not
misleading (Rule 10b-5). This decision had a significant influence on
auditing procedures, and it led to the issuance of SAP Nos. 41 and 47.
Through the use of Rule 10b-5, it may be possible for plaintiffs to cir-
cumvent the defenses of the accountant under Section 18. Managements
have been held liable under Rule 10b-5 on numerous occasions, presenting major liability implications for accountants.

An important decision regarding Rule 10b-5 was handed down by
the Supreme Court on March 30, 1976, in the case of *Ernst & Ernst* v.
Hochfelder. [14] This decision seems to place important limitations on the
scope of civil liability for damages under Rule 10b-5. The plaintiffs in the
Hochfelder case had invested in a securities scheme perpetrated by the
president of a brokerage firm. The scheme involved a so-called escrow
fund which was supposed to yield a high rate of interest. In 1968 the
brokerage firm went bankrupt and the president committed suicide,
leaving a suicide note which described the escrow as "spurious." Ernst
& Ernst, who had served as auditors during most of the period, were
sued on the basis of "negligence." The brokerage firm had an office rule
that all mail addressed to the president or to the firm was to be opened
only by the president. The alleged "negligence" consisted of the failure
by Ernst & Ernst to detect and report the alleged lack of internal controls
resulting from the "mail rule." According to the plaintiffs, this was the
key to the fraudulent scheme.

The Supreme Court concluded that "the words, 'manipulative,'
'device,' and 'contrivance' in the statute [Rule 10b-5] clearly show that it
was the Congressional intent to proscribe a type of conduct quite different from negligence, and the use of the word 'manipulative' particularly
connotes intentional or willful conduct designed to deceive or defraud
investors by controlling or artificially affecting the price of securities." [15]

---

[14] CCH *Federal Securities Law Reporter* 95, 479 (U.S. Supreme Court, March 30, 1976).
[15] Allan Kramer, "The Significance of the Hochfelder Decision," *The CPA Journal* (August, 1976), p. 12.

As a result, the Supreme Court dismissed the action against Ernst & Ernst and thereby indicated an approach toward limiting the previously expanding bounds of civil liability under the federal securities law.

In a somewhat related development, the SEC has adopted Exchange Act Regulation 13B-2 which makes it illegal to falsify company records and lie to accountants. Specifically, the new rules prohibit anyone from falsifying company books and records, and prohibit officers and directors of a registrant from making false, misleading, or incomplete statements to accountants in connection with an audit or review of SEC reports. There is no provision that "scienter," i.e., the intent to deceive, must be present for false statements to be illegal. However, the SEC is not concerned with inadvertent and inconsequential errors. The statute does not require perfection but only accuracy "in reasonable detail." Reasonableness is the standard associated with these new rules.

The SEC's rules should provide greater assurance, to both accountants and the public in general, that the issuer's books and records accurately and fairly reflect its transactions. The rules also should help maintain the integrity of the independent audit of financial statements in connection with SEC filings and provide more reliable and complete financial information to investors pursuant to the Exchange Acts. Finally, the rules should help prevent concealment of questionable or illegal corporate payments and practices under the Foreign Corrupt Practices Act of 1977.

Future Legal Issues. The issue of professional liability is not settled. Lawrence E. Nerheim, General Counsel of the SEC, stated that the Commission has never filed an *amicus* brief on behalf of an accountant to prescribe some limit to liability. He states that "perhaps, just perhaps, the time has arrived. But the questions remain: (1) where does the liability stop? And (2) for what kind of conduct or misconduct should the accountant be liable in damages?"[16] These important questions must yet be answered realistically.

Disclosure Requirements

As has been mentioned several times, an essential objective of the SEC is to provide full and fair disclosure of financial and other information for investors. Therefore, it should not be surprising that the SEC has had a significant impact upon the reporting requirements of businesses. Often at the urging or insistence of the SEC, requirements for

---

[16] Lawrence E. Nerheim, *Journal of Accountancy* (December, 1974), p. 10.

both the amount of information disclosed and the extent of detail provided are increasing. Support for this statement was presented in Chapter 4, where the additional reporting requirements for the annual report to shareholders were outlined. In effect, the SEC now requires that information similar to that filed with the SEC on Form 10-K be reported to shareholders.

Segment Reporting by Diversified Companies. Additional evidence of the increase in reporting requirements can be seen by considering the historical development of lines-of-business reporting. During the early- and mid-1960s, many companies which were unrelated in terms of product lines were merging. This caused considerable interest in a proposal to require these diversified companies (often called conglomerates) to report their sales and profits by major segments of the company. Manuel Cohen, then chairman of the SEC, took the lead in advocating this type of reporting. Due to pressure from the SEC, members of the financial community (including the Financial Executives Institute, the Accounting Principles Board, and the National Association of Accountants) conducted studies concerning the desirability and feasibility of reporting by segments of diversified companies. While the actual recommendations for disclosing segmental information initially came from groups other than the SEC, most notably the FEI, they were prompted by the SEC. In 1969, amendments to Forms S-1, S-7, S-8, and 10 were adopted by the SEC. These amendments required disclosure of sales and profit information by lines of business. Later these requirements were extended to the 10-K and, as mentioned earlier, are now incorporated in the annual reports to shareholders.

In 1976, the Financial Accounting Standards Board issued Statement No. 14, "Financial Reporting for Segments of a Business Enterprise," which required corporations to disclose certain financial information by industry segment and geographic area. Under Statement No. 14, segment disclosures are to be made for each fiscal year for which a complete set of financial statements is presented. Thus, in most cases, two-year comparative segment data should be shown.

The following year, the SEC adopted ASR No. 236 to conform SEC reporting to the requirements established by FASB Statement No. 14. However, the reporting requirements adopted by the SEC, among the first to be incorporated in regulation S-K, still differ somewhat from those of Statement No. 14. The SEC requires that segment revenue, operating profit, and asset information be presented for five years. Thus, the SEC continues to be a strong force in shaping the course of accounting disclosures. As an illustration, Exhibit 5-1 on page 119 shows the segment information presented by General Mills in their 1978 annual report to shareholders. This is essentially the same information as that shown in their 10-K report.

EXHIBIT 5-1

GENERAL MILLS
PRODUCT SEGMENT DATA

Sales

From Continuing Operations Fiscal Year by Major Product Segment (In Millions)	1978		1977		1976		1975		1974	
	Amount	%	Amount	%	Amount	%	Amount	%	Amount	%
Food Processing	$1,861.6	57.4	$1,734.7	62.3	$1,633.6	64.5	$1,519.8	68.8	$1,344.1	70.3
Restaurant Activities	354.9	10.9	240.9	8.7	180.7	7.1	113.6	5.1	77.8	4.1
Crafts, Games and Toys	492.3	15.2	403.3	14.5	347.6	13.7	302.2	13.7	250.7	13.1
Apparel, Accessories, Specialty Retailing and Other.	534.2	16.5	403.9	14.5	371.9	14.7	273.3	12.4	239.4	12.5
Total Sales from Continuing Operations	**$3,243.0**	**100.0**	**$2,782.8**	**100.0**	**$2,533.8**	**100.0**	**$2,208.9**	**100.0**	**$1,912.0**	**100.0**

Earnings

From Continuing Operations Fiscal Year by Major Product Segment (In Millions)	1978		1977		1976		1975		1974	
	Amount	%	Amount	%	Amount	%	Amount	%	Amount	%
Food Processing	$ 169.0	53.5	$ 163.2	58.8	$ 153.2	62.1	$ 132.5	68.0	$ 126.7	66.5
Restaurant Activities	35.9	11.4	25.7	9.2	23.6	9.6	15.1	7.7	8.2	4.3
Crafts, Games and Toys	62.7	19.9	52.4	18.9	41.6	16.9	30.6	15.7	26.8	14.0
Apparel, Accessories, Specialty Retailing and Other.	48.0	15.2	36.3	13.1	28.2	11.4	16.8	8.6	28.9	15.2
Total Operating Profits from Continuing Operations	**$ 315.6**	**100.0**	**$ 277.6**	**100.0**	**$ 246.6**	**100.0**	**$ 195.0**	**100.0**	**$ 190.6**	**100.0**
Unallocated corporate expenses, exclusive of items shown below	(36.2)		(29.0)		(19.3)		(15.5)		(16.7)	
Interest expense	(29.3)		(25.7)		(28.7)		(35.6)		(28.1)	
Profit-sharing distribution	(4.9)		(4.2)		(3.5)		(3.0)		(3.8)	
Total Earnings from Continuing Operations Before Taxes	**$ 245.2**		**$ 218.7**		**$ 195.1**		**$ 140.9**		**$ 142.0**	

Operating profits reported above indicate the relative contributions of General Mills' diversified operations to total earnings. They are not necessarily comparable to similar data from other companies since accounting practices may vary. Variations between the sales and operating profits shown in these tables and similar amounts published in preceding reports are due principally to restatements and minor adjustments in the classification of certain items.

Source: 1978 Annual Report

Lease Reporting. Another example of the SEC's influence upon reporting requirements deals with leases. Over the ten-year period ending June 30, 1973, the APB issued four opinions (Nos. 5, 7, 27, and 31) dealing with leases. Notwithstanding this activity by the accounting profession, in 1973 the SEC issued ASR No. 147 (which required disclosures that went beyond those already provided in the APB opinions). In effect, the SEC required disclosure of the impact on net income as if noncapitalized leases were capitalized. This information was to be footnoted in the financial statements. With the understanding that the FASB also had the topic under consideration, ASR No. 147 contained this paragraph:

> The Commission does not intend by adopting these amendments to prejudge the issues of lease accounting now being considered by the Financial Accounting Standards Board. At such time as that body develops improved standards of accounting for leases, the Commission expects to reconsider the disclosure requirements set forth herein.

In 1976, the FASB issued Statement No. 13, "Accounting for Leases," which superseded APB Opinion Nos. 5, 6, 27, and 31. In effect, the FASB required that leases which are the equivalent of long-term debt (i.e., "finance" leases) must be listed as an obligation on the balance sheet. Statement No. 13 did not take effect immediately, however. During the years 1977-1980, only new leases needed to be placed on the balance sheet; after 1980, FASB Statement No. 13 required retroactive application and all such lease arrangements were to be shown on the balance sheet.

In 1977, the SEC issued ASR No. 225 in an effort to conform its lease accounting and disclosure requirements to those standards adopted by the FASB in Statement No. 13. However, the SEC overruled the FASB with respect to one provision, requiring that by December 24, 1978, all present and past leases must be on the balance sheet.

Whether such disclosures are appropriate and what modifications are still needed continue to be debatable, but the point is that the influence of the SEC on disclosure requirements is significant and pervasive.

Inflation Accounting. The topic of inflation accounting presents another interesting example of the influence and interaction of the SEC and the business community. To provide for investors information which would help them understand the current costs of operating a particular business, the SEC issued ASR No. 190. This release requires the disclosure of certain replacement cost information, including the current replacement costs of inventories and productive capacity and the amount of depreciation based on current costs.

At the time ASR No. 190 was issued, the FASB had proposed price-level adjustments as a possible means of accounting for inflation. However, the SEC's action forced the FASB to reconsider its position. The FASB has published an exposure draft on "Financial Reporting and Changing Prices" which incorporates aspects of both price-level adjustments and current value accounting. Managements of many companies feel that the experience with the SEC's replacement cost has not been positive and that it has been expensive. However, there is opposition to the FASB's proposal as well. At this point it is not clear how the accounting profession will eventually resolve the problems of accounting for inflation. It is almost certain, however, that the SEC's influence will be apparent in resolving this important issue.

The information presented for IBM Corporation in Exhibit 5-2 beginning below will provide an example of replacement cost information. As a contrast, current value data are presented for Days Inns of America, Inc., in Exhibit 5-3 on pages 124-126. Days Inns is one of the few U.S. Companies to date to report such data in the annual report to shareholders.

EXHIBIT 5-2

IBM CORPORATION
NOTES TO CONSOLIDATED FINANCIAL STATEMENTS

Note 18–Replacement Cost Data (Unaudited):

In accordance with Securities and Exchange Commission requirements, estimates of the current replacement cost of inventories and plant, rental machines and other property at December 31, 1978, together with estimated cost of sales, cost of rentals and services and depreciation for the year then ended on the basis of current replacement costs are provided.

Replacement costs are estimates of costs that would be incurred if assets on hand at December 31, 1978, were replaced, and should not be interpreted to be current value or the price for which the assets could be sold. Estimates require numerous subjective judgments and assumptions and, accordingly, the replacement cost data may not be comparable to that of other companies, even those in the same industry. Such data should not be considered indicative of the actual manner or cost of replacement, as any such replacement would take place over a number of years and at costs which would most likely differ from current estimates. In addition, foreign currency exchange rates may change from those rates utilized in these estimates.

Possible operating cost savings which could result from replacement of productive capacity with assets of improved technology and productivity were not included in the

EXHIBIT 5-2 Continued

replacement cost data, as such savings cannot be reasonably quantified, nor has any adjustment been made for investment tax credits that could result from such replacement.

While the company's operating results have been subjected to the pressures of worldwide inflation over the past several years, it has been able to counteract some of the effects of inflation through increased productivity, emphasis on cost and expense controls and selective price increases.

Given the above, in IBM's view, the following estimated replacement cost data should not be used to impute the effect of inflation on the company's net earnings as reported or to develop a restated statement of financial position.

	1978		1977	
	Per financial statements	Estimated replacement cost	Per financial statements	Estimated replacement cost
	(Millions of Dollars)			
At end of year:				
Inventories	$ 1,561	$ 1,601	$ 994	$ 1,008
Plant, rental machines and other property:				
Plant and other property	$ 7,435	$11,746	$ 6,342	$ 9,747
Less accumulated depreciation	3,212	5,416	2,837	4,553
	4,223	6,330	3,505	5,194
Rental machines and parts	11,740	12,312	10,729	11,002
Less accumulated depreciation	6,661	6,419	6,345	5,993
	5,079	5,893	4,384	5,009
Total	$ 9,302	$12,223	$ 7,889	$10,203
For the year:				
Cost of sales	$ 2,838	$ 2,835	$ 2,256	$ 2,239
Cost of rentals and services	$ 4,646	$ 4,566	$ 4,042	$ 3,980
Depreciation charged to:				
Rental machines	$ 246	$ 249	$ 193	$ 196
Cost of sales, rentals and services	1,406	1,348	1,402	1,371
All other expense	418	427	404	424
Total charged to costs and expenses	1,824	1,775	1,806	1,795
Total	$ 2,070	$ 2,024	$ 1,999	$ 1,991

Replacement cost data have been compiled on the assumption that inventories and plant, rental machines and other property were replaced at December 31, 1978. Depreciation based on estimated replacement cost was calculated on the straight-line depre-

EXHIBIT 5-2 Continued

ciation method, as required by the SEC, utilizing the same service lives as for historical cost depreciation. Accumulated depreciation was restated on the basis of the year of addition. Replacement cost data relating to non-U.S. operations were translated at year-end exchange rates for assets and average rates of exchange prevailing during the year for costs and expenses.

The replacement cost of inventory items was estimated by applying the latest available actual or estimated costs, or by application of appropriate price indexes. Unreimbursed expenditures under government contracts amounting in the aggregate to $112 million for 1978 and $98 million for 1977, have been included at historical cost.

The replacement cost of depreciable land improvements and buildings was estimated by applying to each facility, based on its geographical location, appropriate building construction cost indexes. Land and non-depreciable land improvements, buildings under construction and certain assets which are not to be replaced amounting in the aggregate to $722 million for 1978 and $597 million for 1977, have been included at historical cost.

The replacement cost of certain major items of plant and laboratory equipment, some of which are manufactured by or unique to IBM, which would be replaced by technologically advanced equipment, was obtained by means of engineering estimates or by recent vendor quotations. If such replacement would result in a change in productive capacity, appropriate cost adjustments were made. Remaining plant and laboratory equipment, as well as office equipment, was restated by use of indexes appropriate to such equipment categories. Equipment in process has been included at historical cost of $425 million for 1978 and $314 million for 1977.

Rental machine assets were grouped by function and were revalued for replacement cost purposes using the latest representative cost of each group adjusted for performance and capacity. In this manner, the estimated replacement cost gives effect to the significant technological advances which have been characteristic of the industry. Rental machine parts were restated using the method described for rental machines or for inventories, as applicable.

Cost of rental machines sold was determined using the method applied to rental machine assets. Cost of other equipment sales was determined by use of the method described for inventories. Costs totaling $581 million in 1978 and $518 million in 1977, primarily costs of government contracts, have been included at historical cost.

Cost of rentals and services was restated to reflect estimated replacement cost, including the impact of replacement cost depreciation. Costs totaling $318 million in 1978 and $302 million in 1977, primarily taxes on rental machines and write-offs related to rental machines, were included at historical cost.

EXHIBIT 5-3

BALANCE SHEETS (HISTORICAL COST) AND STATEMENTS OF CURRENT VALUES

Days Inns of America, Inc.

	September 30, 1978	
	Statement of Current Values	Balance Sheet (Historical Cost)
Assets		
Current assets:		
Cash (restricted)..	$ 92,000	$ 92,000
Certificates of deposit......................................	3,003,000	3,003,000
Accounts and notes receivable net of allowance for doubtful accounts of $927,000 and $897,000 (Notes 2 and 6):		
Affiliated companies...................................	186,000	186,000
Non-affiliated franchisees.............................	1,504,000	1,504,000
Other..	816,000	816,000
Retail inventories and supplies............................	1,484,000	1,484,000
Prepaid expenses (Note 6).................................	637,000	637,000
Total current assets..............................	7,722,000	7,722,000
Property and equipment (Notes 4, 5 and 7).....................	81,149,000	56,750,000
Less: Accumulated depreciation...........................		(18,984,000)
Accounts and notes receivable:		
Stockholders and affiliated companies (Notes 6 and 8)....	4,821,000	4,821,000
Non-affiliated franchisees and other......................	346,000	346,000
Franchise agreements......................................	15,500,000	
Deferred charges..	802,000	802,000
Accumulated income tax prepayments (Note 8)...............	127,000	127,000
Other assets..	58,000	58,000
	$110,525,000	$51,642,000
Liabilities and Stockholders' Equity		
Current liabilities:		
Notes payable (Notes 4 and 7).............................	$ 3,728,000	$ 3,838,000
Accounts payable..	3,078,000	3,078,000
Accrued expenses and other liabilities....................	2,802,000	2,802,000
Income taxes payable (Note 8).............................	722,000	722,000
Total current liabilities..........................	10,330,000	10,440,000
Notes payable, due after one year (Notes 4 and 7).............	32,578,000	34,157,000
Accounts and notes payable to stockholders and affiliated companies, due after one year (Note 6)...........................	1,520,000	1,520,000
Deferred income taxes (Note 8)..............................		
Income taxes on realization of estimated current values......	17,900,000	
Real estate commissions on realization of estimated current values........	2,900,000	
Deferred income and deposits...............................	868,000	868,000
Stockholders' equity (Notes 5 and 9):		
Common stock, without par value — 1,000,000 shares authorized, 341,670 shares issued............................	59,000	59,000
Capital surplus...	949,000	949,000
Retained earnings...	4,590,000	4,590,000
Unrealized appreciation...................................	39,772,000	
	45,370,000	5,598,000
Less: Treasury stock, at cost — 19,320 and 6,000 shares.....	941,000	941,000
Total stockholders' equity..........................	44,429,000	4,657,000
Commitments and contingent liabilities (Notes 5 and 10)		
	$110,525,000	$51,642,000

EXHIBIT 5-3 Continued

	September 30, 1977	
	ement of rrent lues	Balance Sheet (Historical Cost)
86,000		$ 86,000
576,000		576,000
593,000		593,000
156,000		1,156,000
530,000		530,000
742,000		1,742,000
930,000		930,000
613,000		5,613,000
354,000		52,253,000
		(14,002,000)
867,000		4,867,000
300,000		300,000
000,000		
01,000		1,101,000
70,000		170,000
05,000		$50,302,000
21,000		$4,263,000
543,000		2,543,000
249,000		2,249,000
405,000		405,000
18,000		9,460,000
008,000		35,456,000
14,000		2,114,000
68,000		68,000
300,000		
50,000		
740,000		740,000
59,000		59,000
949,000		949,000
870,000		1,870,000
843,000		
21,000		2,878,000
14,000		414,000
07,000		2,464,000
05,000		$50,302,000

3700 FIRST NATIONAL BANK TOWER
ATLANTA, GEORGIA 30303
404-658-1800

November 22, 1978

To the Board of Directors
and Stockholders of
Days Inns of America, Inc.

Report on Financial Statements (Historical Cost)

In our opinion, the accompanying balance sheets (historical cost) and the related statements of income, of stockholders' equity and of changes in financial position present fairly the financial position of Days Inns of America, Inc. at September 30, 1978 and 1977, and the results of its operations and the changes in its financial position for the years then ended, in conformity with generally accepted accounting principles applied on a consistent basis after restatement for the change explained in Note 9 to the financial statements. Our examinations of these statements were made in accordance with generally accepted auditing standards and accordingly included such tests of the accounting records and such other auditing procedures as we considered necessary in the circumstances.

Report on Statements of Current Values

In addition to the foregoing examination we have applied additional audit procedures in connection with the Statements of Current Values of Days Inns of America, Inc. as of September 30, 1978 and 1977. Our additional procedures included (1) tests of the 1978 and 1977 operating and financial information furnished to Landauer Associates, Inc. for their use in reviewing the Company's estimate of current values, (2) tests of the compilation of the current value data, (3) discussion with Company officials, and (4) a reading of all the estimates of current value included in the Company appraisal reports and a comparison of the assets and liabilities included therein with those included in the balance sheets (historical cost).

The Statements of Current Values provide relevant information about assets and liabilities of the Company which is not provided by the historical cost financial statements and which differs significantly from the historical cost amounts required by generally accepted accounting principles. The accompanying Statements of Current Values should be read in conjunction with the September 30, 1978 and 1977 financial statements (historical cost) and notes thereto.

In our opinion, the Statements of Current Values of Days Inns of America, Inc. as of September 30, 1978 and 1977 have been prepared on the basis described in the accompanying Note to Statements of Current Values.

Price Waterhouse & Co.

EXHIBIT 5-3 Continued

NOTE TO STATEMENTS OF CURRENT VALUES

Days Inns of America, Inc.   *September 30, 1978 and 1977*

The Statements of Current Values provide relevant information about the assets and liabilities of the Company which is not provided by traditional financial statements (historical cost basis). Although current values differ significantly from the historical cost amounts required by generally accepted accounting principles, the management of the Company believes that such information is useful to the readers of its financial statements.

Management's estimates of current values were reviewed and analyzed by Landauer Associates, Inc., real estate consultants, whose letter of concurrence accompanies this note.

The Statements of Current Values do not represent the estimated liquidation value of the Company; rather, the values estimated to be realizable in an orderly disposition of the Company's individual assets and liabilities under the willing buyer/willing seller concept. The values of the interest in its various properties is the estimated current investment which investors would make to purchase the Company's interest in each property's future cash flow.

Management's estimates of unrealized appreciation of $39,772,000 and $25,643,000 at September 30, 1978 and 1977, respectively, are summarized as follows:

| | September 30, | | | |
| | 1978 | | 1977 | |
	Current Values	Historical Cost Basis	Current Values	Historical Cost Basis
Property and equipment interests:				
Motels owned and leased to others.	$26,625,000	$15,585,000	$29,976,000	$19,327,000
Motels and other facilities leased from others (including motels subleased).	37,521,000	8,900,000	23,970,000	8,836,000
Motel capital lease.	3,861,000	2,559,000	3,020,000	2,638,000
Office building, warehouse and travel trailer park.	5,828,000	5,513,000	5,460,000	5,349,000
Motels owned and operated.	6,333,000	4,228,000	1,960,000	1,133,000
Unimproved land.	981,000	981,000	968,000	968,000
	81,149,000		65,354,000	
Franchise agreements.	15,500,000		13,000,000	
	96,649,000		78,354,000	
Historical cost basis.	(37,766,000)	$37,766,000	(38,251,000)	$38,251,000
Income taxes on realization of estimated current values.	(17,900,000)		(12,600,000)	
Real estate commissions on realization of estimated current values.	(2,900,000)		(2,350,000)	
	38,083,000		25,153,000	
Current value reduction in notes payable.	1,689,000		490,000	
Unrealized appreciation.	$39,772,000		$25,643,000	
A reconciliation of unrealized appreciation for the years ended September 30, 1978 and 1977 is as follows:				
Unrealized appreciation at beginning of year.	$25,643,000		$21,430,000	
Increase (decrease) during the year:				
Leasehold interests.	14,407,000		2,087,000	
Leased fee interests and notes payable.	1,590,000		936,000	
Franchise agreements.	2,500,000		3,500,000	
Motels owned and operated.	1,278,000		(12,000)	
Other.	204,000		(48,000)	
Additional costs of disposition.	(5,850,000)		(2,250,000)	
Unrealized appreciation at end of year.	$39,772,000		$25,643,000	

Management Disclosures. The SEC has focused increasing attention on management disclosures, reflecting an effort to meet the objective of preventing fraud and providing full and fair disclosures to investors. For example, one area of concern is that of corporations' expenditures relating to management. The SEC's interest in this area appears to be an outgrowth of problems involving questionable or illegal payments made by many publicly held companies.

In amendments to Regulation S-K, effective beginning in 1979, the SEC expanded its disclosure requirements relating to management remuneration. Under these rules, detailed remuneration must be disclosed for all officers and directors as a group and the five highest-paid executive officers or directors whose total remuneration exceeds $50,000 for the year. In addition, expenditures made for an executive's personal benefit or for purposes unrelated to company business (known as perquisites, or PERKS) must be disclosed. Examples of PERKS include personal use of corporate assets, payment of personal living expenses by a corporation, certain corporate loans, and professional services provided with respect to purely personal matters. Additional personal information is required about directors of companies and executives officers, and any significant indebtedness of management.

Managements are also being asked to provide more information by way of analysis and interpretation of the results of company activities. Exhibit 4-15 on pages 92 and 93 shows the type of information presented by one company in analyzing its summary of earnings. Exhibit 5-4 on pages 128 through 131 provides another example of such explanatory comments by management.

Finally, it appears that the SEC is moving toward requiring company managements to make explicit statements concerning the adequacy of their internal accounting control systems. Such statements will likely require auditor "association" with the reports of management. This is perhaps as important an area of future development as any on the horizon. The Foreign Corrupt Practices Act of 1977 provided the initial impetus for requiring better internal accounting control systems. Now managements are being required to report on the adequacy of such systems. In the future, it is likely that auditors will be required to attest to the adequacy of the internal control systems rather than just review them as a part of the audit examination.

SEC Disclosure Recommendations. Sometimes the SEC does not require disclosures as such, but strongly encourages reporting companies and accountants to present certain information. Such is the case with ASR No. 166, which urges companies in their financial statements

EXHIBIT 5-4

COMPARISON OF ACTUAL TO PROJECTED INCOME AND STOCKHOLDERS' EQUITY

Days Inns of America, Inc.

	For the year ended September 30, 1978		
	Actual	Projected	Variance
Net revenue:			
Lodging	$ 44,242,000	$ 41,202,000	$ 3,040,000
Food, gasoline and novelties	36,896,000	33,445,000	3,451,000
Franchise fees — initial	337,000	343,000	(6,000)
— recurring	7,757,000	6,821,000	936,000
Rental income	3,766,000	3,661,000	105,000
Other income	1,885,000	2,256,000	(371,000)
	94,883,000	87,728,000	7,155,000
Costs and expenses:			
Cost of food, gasoline and novelties	25,234,000	22,115,000	3,119,000
Selling, general, administrative and operating expenses	46,587,000	43,747,000	2,840,000
Rental expense	10,197,000	10,342,000	(145,000)
Depreciation and amortization	5,309,000	4,844,000	465,000
Interest expense net of interest income	3,476,000	3,616,000	(140,000)
	90,803,000	84,664,000	6,139,000
Income before provision for income taxes	4,080,000	3,064,000	1,016,000
Provision for income taxes	1,260,000	915,000	345,000
Net income	$ 2,820,000	$ 2,149,000	$ 671,000
Stockholders' equity	$ 4,657,000	$ 4,086,000	$ 571,000
Occupancy	72.8%	72.0%	.8%
Average room rate	$16.02	$14.92	$1.10
Number of franchise motel openings	9	20	(11)
Total rooms in chain	42,305	42,100	205

EXHIBIT 5-4 Continued

Comments on 1978 Results of Operations

Overview

Operating results for the year ended September 30, 1978, exceeded the projections as set forth in the 1977 annual report. Both revenues and net income exceeded projections and provided additional funds for property improvements. Comments on significant variances from projections are highlighted below.

Revenue

The increase in lodging revenue is attributable to a higher average room rate which resulted from rate increases during the year. Revenue, and the related cost of sales, for food, gas, and novelties are summarized as follows:

(000's Omitted)

	Food		Gasoline		Novelties	
	Actual	Projection	Actual	Projection	Actual	Projection
Revenue	$14,646	$14,117	$18,457	$15,825	$3,793	$3,503
Cost of sales	5,425	5,125	16,851	14,526	2,958	2,464
Gross profit	$ 9,221	$ 8,992	$ 1,606	$ 1,299	$ 835	$1,039
Cost of sales	37.0%	36.3%	91.3%	91.8%	78.0%	70.3%
Revenue per rented room	$5.43	$5.23	$6.84	$5.86	$1.41	$1.30

Gasoline sales exceeded those projected due to public acceptance of the self-serve program. The decrease in the gross profit margin for novelties resulted from an aggressive program to lower inventory levels and eliminate aged merchandise.

Recurring franchise fees for royalties, reservations, and advertising assessments showed a significant improvement over projection, reflecting the improvement in volume and average room rate at franchise locations.

The decrease in other income resulted from a reduction in the size and frequency of conventions held by September Days Club.

Selling, general, administrative and operating expenses

Key expense categories and major variances are noted below (000's omitted).

	Actual	Projection	Variance
Salaries and benefits	$18,902	$18,881	$ 21
Repairs and maintenance	3,201	2,234	967
Utilities	7,270	7,235	35
Advertising	2,281	2,006	275
Professional fees	1,673	1,239	434
Operating supplies	1,540	1,288	252
Travel and entertainment	949	755	194
Postage and printing	983	810	173
			$2,351

Expenditures for the repair and maintenance program were expanded due to the cash flow generated by higher revenues. Including capital replacements and betterments, expenditures totalled $6,706,000 as compared to $5,121,000 projected.

During the year, an advertising program of national scope was instituted resulting in advertising expenses exceeding the amount projected.

Professional fees were influenced by expanded use of computer services, other consulting fees, and additional costs of a labor control program. This program provided the ability to absorb a major increase in the minimum wage rate with less than a 5% increase in total salaries over 1977.

Operating supplies exceeded those projected because of an expanded decor program and resulting purchase of new china, table and flatware.

Travel costs increased over projection as a result of the efforts to insure greater conformity to standards and policies at the motels.

General Comment on Projected Results of Operations 1979-1983

These projections are based on assumptions concerning future events and circumstances. The assumptions disclosed herein are those which management believes are significant to the projections or are key factors upon which financial results depend. Some assumptions inevitably may not materialize and unanticipated events and circumstances may occur subsequent to September 30, 1978. Therefore, the actual results achieved during the projection period may vary from the projections and the variations may be material.

It is expected that prices paid for goods and services and those charged to customers will continue to increase at an inflationary rate of between 5% and 10%. It is also expected that volume increases will occur in room occupancy and food, gasoline and novelty sales.

The Days Inns chain expects to expand in its current market area as well as in new market areas. The bulk of this expansion is projected to be in franchised properties. Additionally, it is assumed the Company will open and operate 3 motels each year beginning in 1980. The strategy will be to locate motels in two areas; 1) at selected sites within existing geographic areas where a void exists, and 2) in new geographic areas where motels will serve to form a base and further expand the franchise program.

Assumptions Utilized by Management in Preparation of These Projections

Lodging revenues are based upon 1) an average occupancy of 76% in 1979 with a one percent increase each year through 1983, 2) an increase of approximately $.50 per year in the average room rate, and 3) an increase of three Company operated sites per year beginning in 1980.

EXHIBIT 5-4 Continued

STATEMENTS OF PROJECTED INCOME AND STOCKHOLDERS' EQUITY

			For the years ending September 30,		
	1979	1980	1981	1982	1983
Net revenue:					
Lodging.	$ 46,185,000	$ 49,868,000	$ 53,808,000	$ 57,936,000	$ 62,256,000
Food, gasoline and novelties.	40,362,000	44,810,000	49,327,000	54,261,000	59,605,000
Franchise fees — initial.	540,000	648,000	760,000	872,000	984,000
— recurring.	9,000,000	10,157,000	11,748,000	13,717,000	15,868,000
Rental income.	4,223,000	4,985,000	5,078,000	2,795,000	2,896,000
Other income.	2,525,000	2,988,000	3,155,000	3,302,000	3,472,000
	102,835,000	113,456,000	123,876,000	132,883,000	145,081,000
Costs and expenses:					
Cost of food, gasoline and novelties.	27,342,000	30,222,000	32,880,000	36,015,000	39,391,000
Selling, general, administrative and operating expenses.	50,828,000	56,058,000	61,549,000	67,418,000	73,507,000
Rental expense.	10,258,000	10,344,000	10,344,000	10,000	10,000
Depreciation and amortization.	5,215,000	5,604,000	6,076,000	9,231,000	9,918,000
Interest expense net of interest income.	3,337,000	3,779,000	4,257,000	10,804,000	11,001,000
	96,980,000	106,007,000	115,106,000	123,478,000	133,827,000
Income before provision for income taxes.	5,855,000	7,449,000	8,770,000	9,405,000	11,254,000
Provision for income taxes.	2,251,000	2,922,000	3,563,000	3,774,000	4,630,000
Net income.	$ 3,604,000	$ 4,527,000	$ 5,207,000	$ 5,631,000	$ 6,624,000
Stockholders' equity.	$ 8,261,000	$ 12,788,000	$ 17,995,000	$ 17,704,000	$ 24,328,000
Occupancy.	76%	77%	78%	79%	80%
Average room rate.	$16.59	$17.00	$17.50	$18.00	$18.50
Number of franchise motel openings.	20	25	30	35	40
Total rooms in chain.	44,900	48,700	53,200	58,200	63,900

EXHIBIT 5-4 Continued

Food, gasoline and novelty sales are projected on the basis of revenue per rented room with annual increases of approximately 5%. Food costs will remain constant at 35% of sales; gasoline costs will decrease slightly; and novelty costs will decrease from 72% in 1979 to 60% in 1983, based on improved inventory controls and revised purchasing procedures.

Initial franchise fees are based on a projected opening fee of $17,400 each, as well as additions to existing sites, conversions of other motels, ownership transfers, and site inspections. Recurring franchise fees are based upon the increased rooms available using approximately the same occupancy and average room rates as for Company operated locations. No recurring franchise fees are included from affiliates.

Selling, general, administrative and operating costs are projected to increase 5% to 10% per year including appropriate changes in the minimum wage rate. Initial advertising and start-up costs of $300,000 a year for additional Company operated sites are projected for 1980 through 1983. Site expenses and home office expenses are projected to increase ratably by a total of approximately 47% and 34%, respectively, from 1979 to 1983.

Beginning in 1982, substantially all lease agreements will be capitalized in accordance with Financial Accounting Standard No. 13 — Accounting for Leases (FAS 13). Accordingly, the projections for the years 1982 and 1983 reflect capitalization of such agreements in effect as of September 30, 1978. Capitalization of such leases results in a decrease in net income of $333,000 and $221,000 in 1982 and 1983, respectively. The cumulative effect on stockholders' equity at September 30, 1982 is a decrease of $5,922,000. Rental income and expense, depreciation, and interest expense have been appropriately presented in accordance with FAS 13 for 1982 and 1983. If the provisions of FAS 13 had been adopted at September 30, 1978, the effect of capitalizing the Company's leases would be to decrease projected net income by $471,000, $370,000, and $322,000 in 1979 through 1981, respectively.

Rental income from leased motels is based upon agreements in existence at September 30, 1978. In 1978, the Company converted 675 motel and lodge rooms to a retirement community. Projected revenue is based on occupancy levels of 40% in 1979 to 80% in 1983 at expected monthly rental rates. Expenses have been estimated based on operations of similar apartment projects.

Rental expense is calculated based on lease agreements in existence at September 30, 1978, and is shown net of sublease income of $809,000 in 1979 and $789,000 in 1980 and 1981. Income of $789,000 from operating sub-leases is shown in rental income for 1982 and 1983.

Depreciation expense reflects a decrease in depreciable assets at leased properties, an increase in the depreciation of replacements and improvements at Company operated sites, and addition of depreciation for three new sites per year beginning in 1980. The estimated cost for these replacements is approximately $35,000,000 over the next five years and for new Company sites is $20,000,000 for 1980 through 1983.

Interest expense increases in future years due to the financing of the three new sites per year beginning in 1980. All other interest is based on a constant level of debt with repayments offset by additional financing of capital expenditures. Interest income from affiliates will decrease moderately with other interest income increasing based on higher levels of cash available for investment.

Provisions for income taxes are based on applicable tax rates. Investment tax credits are based upon estimated property and equipment additions and construction of new motel properties.

The accounting policies used in the projections are those applied in the financial statements for 1978. The financial statements and accompanying notes for the years ended September 30, 1978 and 1977 should be read in connection with the above projections.

Report of Independent Accountants

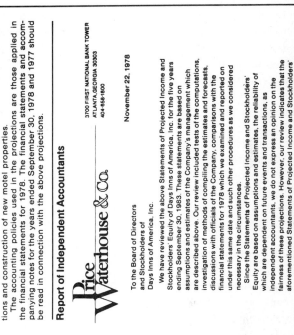

Price Waterhouse & Co.

3700 FIRST NATIONAL BANK TOWER
ATLANTA, GEORGIA 30303
404-658-1600

November 22, 1978

To the Board of Directors
and Stockholders of
Days Inns of America, Inc.

We have reviewed the above Statements of Projected Income and Stockholders' Equity of Days Inns of America, Inc. for the five years ending September 30, 1983. These statements are based on assumptions and estimates of the Company's management which are described above. Our review included tests of the computations, investigation of methods of compiling the estimates and forecasts, discussions with officials of the Company, comparisons with the financial statements for 1978 which we examined and reported on under this same date and such other procedures as we considered necessary in the circumstances.

Since the Statements of Projected Income and Stockholders' Equity are based on assumptions and estimates, the reliability of which are dependent on future events and transactions, as independent accountants, we do not express an opinion on the aforementioned Statements of Projected Income and Stockholders' Equity were compiled on the basis of both the described assumptions of the Company's management and the accounting policies applied in the financial statements for the year 1978.

Price Waterhouse & Co.

to make "substantial and specific disclosure as to significant and increasing business uncertainties." Illustrative of the types of recommended disclosures are situations where there have been substantial changes in marketable securities portfolios, loan portfolios (even where increased provisions for losses have been made), and where a small number of projects may dominate the net effect of operating results. The release states that when unusual circumstances arise or where there are significant changes in the degree of business uncertainty existing in a reporting entity, a registrant has the responsibility of communicating these items in its financial statements.

Another example relates to the disclosure of company projections of future performance. At the present time, the SEC has decided not to require forecasts, but it has adopted Securities Act Guide 62 and Exchange Act Guide 5 which encourage the publication of company projections. If a company elects to present forecast data, it may not present only those items that appear favorable or that might give misleading impressions. Forecasts are not required, but if they are used, the company must follow the guidelines provided by the SEC. The SEC has also established "safe harbor" rules for those associated with forecasts prepared in a reasonable manner and with good faith, again as a means of encouraging the publication of forward-looking information in SEC filings.

An example of reporting projected income data, including management comments and the auditor's statement relating thereto, was presented as Exhibit 5-4 on pages 128-131 for Days Inns of America, Inc.

Regulation

Questions have been raised with respect to whether independent public accounting firms are adequately performing their functions of independent review and attestation. These questions are at least partially the result of a number of failures of publicly owned corporations in the early 1970s that resulted in large losses to investors. To some, the accounting profession appears unable to establish a satisfactory self-regulatory process. Prior to 1977, the AICPA had no real mechanism for regulation of CPA firms. Firms were regulated sporadically by the SEC through its disciplinary powers, or by the courts. By the mid-1970s, however, various sources generated tremendous pressure for the accounting profession to establish an appropriate regulatory framework to monitor and strengthen the quality of work performed by independent accountants.

In an effort to be responsive to the SEC and other critics of the profession, the AICPA took a major step towards self-regulation. In September, 1977, it established two divisions of firms within the AICPA, the SEC Practice Section and the Private Companies Section. The AICPA leadership hoped that a strong self-regulatory program within the SEC Practice Section would satisfy the profession's critics. Requirements for membership in the SEC Practice Section include (1) regular peer reviews every three years, (2) minimum amounts of continuing professional education, (3) adherence to quality control standards for audit practice, (4) adherence to a defined scope of services, (5) a five-year rotation of the primary audit partner on SEC engagements, (6) preissuance review of reports on SEC engagements, (7) reports to the audit committee or board of directors concerning disagreements with management, and (8) maintenance of minimum amounts of liability insurance. Various sanctions can be placed on member firms who fail to maintain the requirements. The activities of the SEC Practice Section are reviewed by a Public Oversight Board which reports to the SEC and to the public.

Perhaps the most important accomplishment of the AICPA in its self-regulatory program is the peer review program.[17] The objective of a peer review is to express an opinion as to whether a firm's system of quality control provides the firm with reasonable assurance of conforming with professional standards. Reviews may be conducted either by a committee-appointed review team or by an independent member firm. A peer review involves (1) a study and evaluation of the review firm's system of quality control and (2) tests of compliance with the firm's quality control policies and procedures. The review team then submits a report and letter of comments regarding areas that may require corrective action to the review firm and the AICPA.

Whether the profession will be permitted to continue regulating itself or whether regulation will be mandated by Congress or the SEC is still a matter of question. A call for direct government regulation has come from Congressman Moss (D-California). In June, 1978, he introduced a bill which would establish a National Organization of Securities and Exchange Commission Accountancy (NOSECA), under the direct authority and control of the SEC, to regulate the accounting profession. The SEC, however, in a report to Congress in July, 1978, supported the AICPA's efforts at self-regulation and concluded that the Commission "is not at this time convinced that comprehensive direct government regulation of accounting or accountants would afford the public either

---

[17] J. Michael Cook and Haldon G. Robinson, "Peer Review: The Accounting Profession's Program," *The CPA Journal* (March, 1979).

increased protection or a more meaningful basis for confidence in the work of public accountants. "[18] The Commission emphasized, however, that additional and ongoing progress is needed for its continuing support.

Development of Accounting Principles

The Commission's official philosophy has been, from the beginning, to allow the accounting profession to develop generally accepted accounting principles. In 1938, ASR No. 4 stated:

> In cases where financial statements filed with this Commission pursuant to its rules and regulations under the Securities Act of 1933 or the Securities Exchange Act of 1934 are prepared in accordance with accounting principles for which there is no substantial authoritative support, such financial statements will be presumed to be misleading or inaccurate despite disclosures contained in the certificate of the accountant or in footnotes to the statements, provided the matters involved are material. In cases where there is a difference of opinion between the Commission and the registrant as to the proper principles of accounting to be followed, disclosure will be accepted in lieu of correction of the financial statements themselves only if the points involved are such that there is substantial authoritative support for the practices followed by the registrant and the position of the Commission has not previously been expressed in rules, regulations or other official releases of the Commission, including the published opinions of its Chief Accountant.

The Commission requirement is twofold. First, to be accepted by the SEC at all, financial statements must be prepared in accordance with accounting principles which have "substantial authoritative support." If the accounting principles used do not have substantial authoritative support, they are presumed *prima facie* false or inaccurate despite any disclosures. Second, if the Commission disagrees with the registrant and the accounting principles used have substantial authoritative support, the SEC will accept footnotes to the statements in lieu of correcting the statements to the SEC view, provided the SEC has not previously expressed its opinion on the matter in published material.

Two points here are critical to an understanding of the relationship of the SEC and accounting principles. First, the SEC reserved the right explicitly (which it would have anyway under its general powers) to rule against a registrant even if it follows principles having substantial authoritative support. Second, the SEC reserved the right to determine

---

[18] *The CPA Letter,* July, 1978, p. 1.

what principles have substantial authoritative support.

Government Involvement. Traditionally, the Commission has looked to the accounting profession to take the lead in developing principles that would have official support. The APB was established by the AICPA to formulate such authoritative principles. In 1973, the FASB replaced the APB as the official policymaking body. As indicated earlier, the FASB received an official vote of confidence from the SEC with ASR No. 150. It states:

> Various Acts of Congress administered by the Securities and Exchange Commission clearly state the authority of the Commission to prescribe the methods to be followed in the preparation of accounts and the form and content of financial statements . . . and the responsibility to assure that investors are furnished with information necessary for informed investment decisions. In meeting this statutory responsibility effectively, in recognition of the expertise, energy and resources of the accounting profession and without abdicating its responsibilities, the Commission has historically looked to the standard setting bodies designated by the profession to provide leadership in establishing and improving accounting principles.

> The body presently designated . . . to establish accounting principles is the Financial Accounting Standards Board (FASB).

> Principles, standards, and practices promulgated by the FASB in its Statements and Interpretations will be considered by the Commission as having substantial authoritative support, and those contrary to such FASB promulgations will be considered to have no such support.

Despite these statements outlining the SEC's desire for the profession to take the lead in developing principles, the Commission has not always expressed unqualified confidence in the profession's ability and performance. Several SEC officials have indicated that the profession has not adequately fulfilled its role in developing accounting principles. A statement by Commissioner Woodside is typical of those somewhat critical of the profession. After stating that the Commission has, in general, followed a policy of allowing the profession to develop principles, he states:

> It may also be that we should have made greater use of our Accounting Series Releases to announce firm policies on more accounting matters.

> Certainly, if the academic and operating branches of the accounting profession continue to join certain analysts and commentators in suggesting the absence of accounting principles and the noncomparability, and therefore the limited usefulness, of corporate financial

statements, it will become increasingly difficult as a policy matter for us to justify and rely upon Accounting Series Release No. 4 and Rule 2-02 of S-X, which governs the contents of a certificate.[19]

Another comment from A. A. Sommer, Jr., a SEC Commissioner, is relevant:

> Very frankly, I am troubled as I read the history of the last forty years' effort of the accounting profession to establish a system of viable accounting principles. The FASB is the third structure created for the purpose; it is the third effort to avoid in the future the disillusionments with financial reporting that have recurred with dismaying frequency; it is the third chance of the profession to prove that the Commission can safely entrust leadership in this task to the profession. These forty years have been characterized by alternating Commission moods of warm confidence in the ability of the profession to do the job and intense criticisms of the failures of the profession.
>
> As one reads this history, and then looks at the continuing problem with adequate financial reporting, one is tempted to conclude that indeed the Commission should undertake a full exercise of its statutory powers and through its own efforts, bring forth a sufficient, workable set of accounting principles.[20]

Considering these criticisms, it is not surprising that some feel a shift from the private to the public sector is taking place. During the period of time in which the APB published its last six opinions, the SEC issued 14 Accounting Series Releases. During the first year of the FASB, the SEC published 20 ASRs, prompting the chairman of the FASB at that time, Marshall S. Armstrong, to remark that the SEC was doing much more than the private sector. In fact, he continued, ASR No. 147 can be viewed as the SEC preempting the private sector in the establishment of the GAAP.[21]

Another leading expert, Leonard M. Savoie, has stated:

> For sentimental reasons I still prefer to see accounting standards set in the private sector, but I can no longer advocate this position with great conviction. My reasons are that standards are now being determined

---

[19] Byron D. Woodside, "Address Before Hayden Stone Accounting Forum," *Journal of Accountancy* (February, 1966), p. 51.

[20] Securities and Exchange Commission, "The SEC and the FASB: Their Roles," news release of January 21, 1974 (Washington: U.S. Government Printing Office, 1974). A. A. Sommer, Jr. delivered this speech at the University of Washington, Seattle, Washington, on January 21, 1974.

[21] Marshall S. Armstrong, reported in *Journal of Accountancy* (March, 1974), pp. 9-10.

largely in the public sector, and inevitably the function will be taken over completely by the public sector. The SEC occupies a dominant position in determining accounting standards and the APB a subordinate one. The FASB will have the identical relationship with the SEC . . . that is, the SEC will be dominant and the FASB will be subordinate.[22]

Others have made the point even more strongly. Professor Charles T. Horngren, a member of the APB from 1969 through 1973, stated:

It is time to dispel the oft-heard myth that a private group is setting the accounting principles which are then enforced by the policing agency, the SEC. The job of devising accounting principles is a joint effort, a private-public institutional arrangement that should be explicitly admitted and publicized forthrightly. . . . Moreover, the constraints affecting both the SEC and the APB should also be recognized.[23]

Even though the SEC possesses legal authority to control accounting procedures and form, most accountants still believe that the development of accounting principles should come almost entirely from within the profession. The truth is, however, that the SEC has had a broad influence in the development of generally accepted accounting principles. The SEC has been described as top management and the accounting profession as the front-line management; when top management dislikes a decision that has been made, the decision is altered. A past chief accountant for the SEC, John C. Burton, disagreed with this position but commented on the possibility of future SEC involvement:

. . . we are in partnership . . . we do not want to be senior partner, although it might turn out that way—depending on how the profession moves.[24]

The cause of increasing involvement by the public sector has been clearly stated by Savoie:

. . . the failure of business and the accounting profession to accept the authority of APB rules and regulations is the main reason its [the SEC] function has moved further into the public sector.[25]

---

[22] Leonard M. Savoie, "Accounting Attitudes," *Financial Executive* (October, 1973), pp. 78-80.

[23] Charles T. Horngren, "Accounting Principles: Private or Public Sector?" *Journal of Accountancy* (May, 1972), p. 39.

[24] "Paper Shuffling and Economic Reality," *Journal of Accountancy* (January, 1973), p. 28.

[25] Savoie, *op. cit.* See also Richard T. Baker, *Financial Executive* (January, 1972), p. 16.

The business community and the accounting profession, by their own hesitance to comply with APB and FASB pronouncements, have apparently brought about increased government involvement in the establishment of GAAP. Thus, only if the FASB responds quickly to problems and if corporate managements and accounting practitioners give credence to the statements of the FASB will the trend be altered.

The Investment Credit. In the Revenue Act of 1962, Congress created a new taxation concept called the investment credit. The investment credit is a certain percentage of the cost of some depreciable assets used to offset income tax payable in the year the assets are purchased. The APB considered the various accounting treatments possible for the investment credit and issued its Opinion No. 2, setting forth what it believed to be the correct method. Basically, the APB decided that the allowable investment credit should be reflected in net income over the productive life of the acquired property and not just in the year in which it was placed in service.

The SEC did not support the APB and it concluded, in ASR No. 97, that two methods would be acceptable. These were (1) essentially the same method proposed by the APB or (2) a method in which a significant percentage of the investment credit would be taken as a reduction of income tax liability in the year of acquisition, the remainder being deferred until future years. This method had been considered and rejected by the APB.

The SEC's position reflected the lack of support by corporate managers and accounting practitioners of the APB action. Many financial statements were subsequently certified even though their treatment of the investment credit was contrary to APB requirements. This happened despite a plea from the AICPA President Robert E. Witschey for AICPA members to qualify their opinions on statements of companies not following the APB position.

In view of the lack of general acceptance of its opinion, in 1964 the APB reconsidered and issued Opinion No. 4 which stated that although it preferred the method outlined in Opinion No. 2, the APB would accept the so-called "full flow-through" method. This method considered the investment credit to be a reduction of taxes in the year of acquisition only. The SEC then issued revised regulations which were substantially (with some differences of form) the same as those of Opinion No. 4.

The last round in the investment credit battle portrayed the impotence of both the APB and the SEC when Congress and public opinion went against them. This series of events lends strong credence to the statement by Professor Horngren that "setting accounting principles is indeed subject to popularity testing."[26]

The investment credit was repealed by Congress but was subsequently reinstated in 1971. The APB issued an exposure draft to its members in October, 1971, after receiving a commitment from the SEC in support of its position and from the Treasury Department to remain neutral. The Senate Finance Committee issued its version of the 1971 Revenue Act in November. In response to lobbying by industry groups, the Finance Committee indicated that companies should be free to choose alternative methods of accounting for the investment credit. Several days later, the Treasury Department sent to the Chairman of the Senate Finance Committee a letter indicating support for a continuation of the optional treatment previously used. Congress then destroyed both the APB and SEC positions by passing legislation that no taxpayer could be required to use any one particular method against personal consent.

Oil and Gas Accounting. A more recent example of SEC influence in the development of accounting principles involves a controversy over oil and gas accounting. The SEC became involved with the question of accounting in the oil and gas industry with the passage of the Energy Policy and Conservation Act (EPCA) in December, 1975. This Act required that the SEC prescribe adequate accounting practices for use by oil and gas producers to assure the development of a reliable energy data base. The Act authorized the SEC to rely on the FASB for the development of these accounting practices, as long as it provided an opportunity for public comments on the FASB's decision and felt assured that oil and gas producers would follow the FASB's rules.

Subsequently, the FASB issued a discussion memorandum, held public hearings, and spent many months in an effort to reconcile the differing opinions and arrive at a standard. Two major views were represented in the oil and gas industry. Advocates of "full-cost" accounting felt that all exploration costs, including the costs associated with dry holes, should be capitalized. The "successful efforts" advocates believed that only those costs directly incurred in the successful recovery of hydrocarbons should be expensed. In general, companies using the "full-cost" approach would show higher earnings with less fluctuation from year to year than those companies using "successful efforts." In December, 1977, the FASB finally issued Statement No. 19, "Financial Accounting and Reporting by Oil and Gas Producing Companies," which required that all oil and gas companies use the "successful efforts" method of accounting.

---

[26] Horngren, *op. cit.*, p. 40.

Immediately, the FASB's rules were actively opposed by many smaller oil and gas companies which used the full-cost method. Those companies objected strongly on the basis that elimination of the full-cost method would seriously impair their ability to obtain financing. The SEC, acting with the responsibility vested by EPCA, reviewed the standard, held hearings, and in August, 1978, concluded that none of the existing methods of oil and gas accounting were adequate, and that a new method called "Reserve Recognition Accounting" should be developed. This new method was to be developed over a three-year period and would be based on the valuation of proven oil and gas reserves. In the interim, the SEC determined (in ASR Nos. 253, 257, and 258) to allow companies to continue using either the successful efforts method or the full-cost method of accounting for oil and gas exploration and production.

This decision, in effect, undercut the authority of FASB Statement No. 19 and represented a serious blow to the profession. Shortly thereafter the FASB issued Statement No. 25 which suspended certain of its requirements and the effective date of Statement No. 19, thus resolving the conflict with the SEC. The SEC, in announcing its decision, emphasized that although its conclusion in this instance differed from the conclusions of the FASB, it did not represent a change in the SEC's basic policy of looking to the FASB for the initiative in establishing and improving accounting standards. The actions of the SEC, however, do represent a challenge to the profession and the business community.

Summary

The private standard-setting bodies do not have the last word on accounting principles, contrary to what many have assumed. Clearly, accounting principles are subject to SEC, industry, and Congressional support. The FASB must be prepared to operate in this environment.

In the author's view, the SEC has significantly influenced the accounting profession and the business community. The SEC's influence is viewed as an important factor in determining generally accepted accounting principles and auditing standards as well as business practices. A continual revitalization of the accounting profession will be necessary if a viable partnership is to be maintained. Commissioner Sommer summarizes the dilemma:

> It seems likely that this tremendous effort (the FASB) we are all about is the last opportunity to keep this job out of the hands of government and, therefore, I think it is important that everyone involved do, in the vernacular, their damndest to make the effort work. This means industry, profession, Commission—for I repeat, another failure will produce

irresistible insistence that the chore be removed to other hands.[27]

The challenge to accountants and business executives is real, exciting, and potentially rewarding.

DISCUSSION QUESTIONS

1. Why has the SEC been given such broad statutory power in relation to accounting principles and procedures?

2. How was the SEC granted this power? Trace the events.

3. What is Regulation S-X? What is Regulation S-K?

4. What are Accounting Series Releases? What is their purpose? How do ASRs differ from SABs (Staff Accounting Bulletins)?

5. Discuss some of the instances in which the SEC has exerted influence upon auditing standards and the significance of these influences.

6. What is the accounting profession's view of fraud detection in an audit? What seems to be the SEC position?

7. What factors have led to the current emphasis upon the legal liability of auditors in connection with publicly issued financial statements? What impact might the Hochfelder case have?

8. In what main areas are accountants' legal liabilities grouped?

9. Why is the SEC involved in disclosure issues? What are some of the primary areas of interest where the SEC has been an important motivator of additional disclosure?

10. What specific steps have been taken by the accounting profession to establish a system of self-regulation?

11. How has the SEC generally elected to fulfill its responsibilities with regard to accounting principles?

12. What seems to be the current trend of the SEC action in regard to accounting principles?

13. Should GAAP be promulgated in the private or public sector?

---

[27] Securities and Exchange Commission, *loc. cit.*

APPENDIX
SELECTED REFERENCES

Primary Sources

1. The Acts as amended, and the guides, rules, and regulations for each of the Acts. The guides, rules, and regulations are official explanations and interpretations of the Acts. Copies of the Acts and the guides, rules, and regulations may be purchased from the Government Printing Office, Washington, DC 20402.

2. Regulation S-X and Regulation S-K. These are the basic documents that explain the form and content of financial statements and nonfinancial statement data to be included in SEC filings and reports. The regulations are amended frequently and care should be taken to ensure proper understanding of the amendments. Copies can be purchased from the Government Printing Office.

3. Accounting Series Releases. The SEC uses the ASRs to explain or clarify any desired changes in accounting or auditing procedures in reports filed with the SEC. A complete list should be maintained as a necessary correlative to SEC-related accounting work.

4. Staff Accounting Bulletins. The SABs provide explanations, interpretations, and procedures used by the staff of the SEC in administering the federal securities laws. They are not "official" pronouncements of the SEC, but contain useful information in dealing with the SEC.

5. Financial Accounting Standards Board Statements and Interpretations. The FASB pronouncements provide the basis for generally accepted accounting practice.

Additional Sources

1. Professional Services

A. *Accountants' SEC Practice Manual* (Chicago: Commerce Clearing House, Inc.) A reference service updated monthly, providing a practical guide in the preparation of SEC reports and registration statements.

B. *Federal Securities Law Reporter* (Chicago: Commerce Clearing House, Inc.) This reference work contains indexes and cross-references and has interpretations of all of the Acts, cases, procedures, and current material.

C. *SEC Compliance* (Englewood Cliffs: Prentice-Hall, Inc.) A monthly bulletin providing an update on all SEC financial reporting and form changes. An excellent resource.

D. *Securities Regulations* (Englewood Cliffs: Prentice-Hall, Inc.) This reference work has indexes and cross-references and contains summaries of all the Acts, cases, and interpretations of procedures and rules. Continual updating is an important feature of this service.

E. Several accounting firms have SEC departments and provide books and manuals for training and informing their staffs. While these materials may be somewhat difficult for the casual student to obtain, the serious researcher will find the accounting firms cooperative and their material useful. In addition, most large accounting firms provide up-to-date information to their clients. Some examples of these reports are:
   (1) *Accounting Events and Trends,* by Price Waterhouse & Co.
   (2) *Executive News Briefs,* by Arthur Andersen & Co.
   (3) *New Developments Summary,* by Alexander Grant & Company
   (4) *Financial Reporting Developments,* by Ernst & Whinney
   (5) *SEC Newsletter,* by Laventhol & Horwath
   (6) *The Week in Review,* by Deloitte, Haskins, & Sells

F. *The CPA Letter* (New York: American Institute of Certified Public Accountants). A semimonthly news report published by the AICPA and containing current events relating to accounting and often SEC reporting.

G. The Practicing Law Institute in New York has sponsored numerous conferences on securities problems. The conferences are reported in equally numerous publications. Check legal libraries for a complete list.

2. Textbooks

There are a number of lengthy technical texts on the SEC. The following is not a comprehensive list, but it will give the serious student an adequate start for research.

A. Bloomenthal, Harold S. *Securities and Federal Corporate Law.* New York: Clark Boardman Co., 1972. This book provides a technical review of the legal problems involved in securities registration. This is a "how-to-do-it" book of instructions for practitioners. Probably found in legal libraries.

B. Bloomenthal, Harold S. (ed.). *Securities Law Review*. New York: Clark Boardman Co., 1978. Each year an additional volume of this series is published. The format is a book of articles on various subjects of interest in the securities field.

C. Jennings, Richard W., and Harold Marsh, Jr. *Securities Regulations: Cases and Material*. Mineola: Foundation Press, 1972. Designed as a classroom case reference, the book is useful for researching cases and their implications. This book is supplemented annually with current material.

D. Lasser, J. K., and J. A. Gerardi. *Federal Securities Act Procedure*. New York: McGraw-Hill Book Co., 1934. Written at the time the Acts were inaugurated, the book provides a contemporary look at the controversy and passage of the securities laws.

E. Loss, Louis. *Securities Regulation*. Boston: Little, Brown & Co., 1961. Professor Loss has not only written the text, but also provides periodic supplements that keep the text current. Explanations of current problems and new procedures are given.

F. McWhirter, Bruce J., (ed.). *Donnelly SEC Handbook*. Chicago: R. R. Donnelly & Sons Company, 1977. A several-volume series containing frequently used statutes, rules, forms, and releases relating to the principal Acts administered by the SEC.

G. Rappaport, Louis H. *SEC Accounting Practice and Procedure*, 3d ed. New York: Ronald Press Co., 1972. Rappaport's treatise on the SEC has proven helpful for many years. The book is thorough, yet easy to read and understand.

H. Robinson, Gerald J., and Klaus Eppler. *Going Public*. New York: Clark Boardman Co., 1974. An explanation of the problems of underwriting. Another "how-to" book for practitioners.

I. Sowards, Hugh L. (ed.). *Business Organizations: The Federal Securities Act*. 2 vols. New York: Matthew Bender & Co., 1973. Another legal approach to understanding securities problems, and it provides a historical background. Again, available in legal libraries. Volume 2 of this series is comprised of seven volumes of technical material.

J. Wiesen, Jeremy L. *Regulating Transactions in Securities*. St. Paul: West Publishing Company, 1975. A brief text on securities regulation.

3. SEC Publications

A. *Annual Reports*. Each fiscal year a summary of SEC activity is given to Congress in an annual report. The reports contain statistical information as well as narrative explanations of procedures and activities. Available from the Government Printing Office or in most university libraries.

B. *News Digest.* A brief summary of financial proposals to and action by the SEC. Useful for an interim review of SEC registrations and actions taken by the SEC.

C. *SEC Docket.* A weekly review of the official releases and statements by the SEC. Contains current cases and litigation together with the disposition of the cases.

D. *The Work of the Securities and Exchange Commission.* This pamphlet gives a brief explanation of the history and function of the Commission.

E. *Statistical Bulletin.* Contains complete statistics on securities traded, market activity, securities offerings, and registrations. A tool for statistical research in securities markets.

F. The SEC commissioner and officers often give speeches to various university and professional groups. These speeches are usually published and are available at most SEC offices. The speeches are one way to keep current on SEC thinking and emphasis.

G. The Commission publishes many additional pamphlets on specific problems and ideas. Most university libraries will have a rather complete set.

4. Periodicals

The list of periodicals containing SEC-related material is endless. The following is a selected list of some that should prove useful.

A. *Financial Analysts Journal.* This professional journal has a monthly section on securities laws and problems. In addition to the summary of current problems, frequent articles explain more carefully the various aspects of securities statutes.

B. *Financial Executive.* Another professional journal that has carried numerous articles on various aspects of securities laws. The articles are well documented and useful for staying abreast of securities problems.

C. *Journal of Accountancy.* A well-known accounting publication, the *Journal* often has articles and comments relative to SEC practice or the interaction of the AICPA and the SEC.

D. *Review of Securities Regulations.* Published by Standard & Poor's Corporation, this work analyzes current laws and regulations affecting the securities industry.

E. *Securities Regulation and Law Report.* A weekly publication of the Bureau of National Affairs, Washington, D.C., designed to inform professionals on current topics and problems.

F. *Securities Regulation and Transfer Report.* This short newsletter, published by Management Reports, Inc., Boston, provides a look at current matters and an explanation of effects on management. Generally available at legal libraries.

G. Most laws schools have periodic "Law Reviews." These publications often have SEC-related articles that are useful sources of current legal explanations.

H. Business periodicals often carry short articles or comments on the SEC. While the articles are not always scholarly, they do inform readers of current, practical matters. Magazines such as *Business Week, Fortune,* and *Nation's Business,* along with the *Wall Street Journal* and the "Business and Finance" section of each Sunday's *New York Times* are useful for the accountant and business person.

I. Several state CPA societies, in addition to the AICPA, publish journals that have articles on the SEC. Check with the professional organization in your state for any additional information that may be available.

J. Many colleges of business publish scholarly journals that provide useful research articles on the SEC. *Harvard Business Review* and *Columbia Journal of World Business* are just two examples. See the periodicals listing at universities for other journals.

5. *Other*

A. Ainsworth, LeRoy G., and Johnny S. Turner. *An Overview of the SEC with a Guide to Researching Accounting-Related SEC Problems.* Provo: Brigham Young University Press, 1971. A small monograph useful in designing research on the SEC.

B. "And Now: The 'Gutsy' Annual Report." *Dun's Review* (March, 1975).

C. Benston, George J. "Evaluation of the Securities Exchange Act of 1934," and A. A. Sommer, Jr. "The Other Side." *Financial Executive* (May, 1974).

D. Brombert, Alan R. *Securities Law: Fraud.* New York: McGraw-Hill Book Co., 1973. This three-volume set provides a historical and current perspective on Rule 10b-5. Recent expansion of fraud detection is discussed and illustrated.

E. Haining, Hazel E. "Federal Regulation of the Securities Industry." Doctoral dissertation, Lincoln, Nebraska, 1972. This provides an examination of the events leading to and some of the results of the federal statutes governing the securities markets.

F. Knauss, Robert L. *Securities Regulation Sourcebook*. New York: Practicing Law Institute, 1972. A single-volume collection of the most important reference materials on securities regulations. The book accomplishes its purpose in a complete but technical way.

G. "The SEC's Crusade on Wall Street." Part I, *Fortune* (November, 1974); Part II, *Fortune* (December, 1974).

DISCUSSION POINTS

CHAPTER 1

1. When the economic system was basically a barter economy, the management and owners of a business were usually the same individuals. External reporting of financial data was not necessary. However, as business activity increased in size and complexity, external financing became more common. This growth of businesses led to extensive use of the corporate form of business; thus, ownership and management became separated. This separation necessitated the need for objective verification of data and created a need for disclosure of information to owners and potential investors. However, there were abuses of trust and losses of invested capital and securities. Thus, the government began to step in and require businesses to publicly disclose their activities.

2. No, the first attempt at securities regulation occurred as early as 1902. However, three major bills which were introduced before 1930 never made it out of committee to either the House or the Senate.

3. Blue-sky laws are state laws aimed at regulating the sale of securities. The categories of these laws were:
   A. Fraud laws which imposed penalties for fraud in the sale of securities
   B. Regulatory laws which prohibited the sale of securities until an application was filed and permission was granted by the state

   These laws were ineffective because:
   A. Laws between states were not consistent.
   B. State legislatures were reluctant to enforce the laws.
   C. State laws contained numerous exemptions.

4. The practices of the 1920s which led to the erosion of the stock market were:
   A. Price manipulation which gave false impressions of market activity and drove prices up, allowing profiteers large gains before prices fell back to their true market values
   B. False and misleading statements which had as their objective the making of profits at the expense of unwary investors
   C. Extensive use of credit (large margins) which produced a slight market decline and started chain reactions which resulted in many investors not being able to cover their margins
   D. Misuse of information by corporate officials or "insiders" which involved the withholding of information until the officers could take

advantage of it

5. The primary function of the SEC is to ensure "full and fair" disclosure of all material facts concerning securities offered for public investment. Its purpose is not to prohibit speculative securities from entering the market, but to insist that investors be provided adequate information in order that they might make an informed decision.

6. Individuals who view the establishment of the SEC as unnecessary do not believe there were sufficient abuses in securities transactions prior to the 1930s to warrant regulatory legislation such as the Securities Acts. They do not believe regulation through an agency such as the SEC was needed. Furthermore, they argue that the information provided through regulatory disclosures is not sufficiently useful to investors to warrant the costs of regulation.

   While the cost-benefit relationship of providing information must be considered carefully, the author accepts the underlying premise of the SEC that regulation of the securities markets is in the public interest and that the disclosure requirements do assist in providing more efficient capital markets.

7. Due to its legal authority to regulate the securities markets, the SEC has significant influence in securities markets activity. If anything, the SEC's role is likely to expand during the next decade.

8. The SEC is directed by five commissioners who are appointed by the President for a five-year term, one member's term expiring each year. Administered from the Washington, D.C., headquarters, the SEC has regional and branch offices in the major financial areas of the U.S. The major divisions of the SEC and their functions are:

   A. Division of Corporation Finance
      1. Assists in establishing and regulating adherence to reporting and disclosure standards
      2. Sets standards for disclosure requirements of proxy solicitations
      3. Provides interpretative and advisory service of requirements to professionals

   B. Division of Market Regulation
      1. Assists in regulation of national securities exchanges and brokers and dealers by attempting to discourage fraud or manipulation with the sale or purchase of securities, and by supervising issuance of new securities
      2. Supervises broker-dealer inspection program

3. Provides interpretative advice to investors and registrants

C. Division of Enforcement
   1. Supervises investigations
   2. Institutes injunctive actions

D. Division of Corporate Regulation
   1. Helps administer the Public Utility Holding Company Act of 1935
   2. Performs the Commission's advisory functions to the U.S. District Courts under Chapter XI of the Bankruptcy Act

E. Division of Investment Management Regulation
   1. Assists the SEC in administering the Investment Company Act of 1940 and the Investment Advisers Act of 1940
   2. Supervises investigations arising from these Acts

9. Regional offices serve as field representatives for the Commission. They have the power to initiate investigations into possible violations and to conduct surprise investigations of brokers and dealers.

10. The Chief Accountant provides the Commission with expert advice in matters of accounting and auditing standards. The Chief Accountant has the statutory power to designate accounting principles and is the main liaison between the SEC and the accounting profession.

CHAPTER 2

1. The primary Acts governed by the SEC are the Securities Act of 1933 and the Securities Exchange Act of 1934. The secondary Acts include: the Public Utility Holding Company Act of 1935, the Trust Indenture Act of 1939, the Investment Company Act of 1940, the Investment Advisers Act of 1940, the National Bankruptcy Act, Chapter XI, the Securities Investor Protection Act of 1970, and the Foreign Corrupt Practices Act of 1977.

2. The basic objectives of the Securities Act of 1933 are:
   A. To provide investors with material financial and other information concerning securities offered for public sale
   B. To prohibit misrepresentation, deceit, and other fraudulent acts and practices in the sale of securities generally (whether or not required to be registered)

These objectives are being met by:
   A. Requiring any firm offering securities for sale to register with the SEC
   B. Imposing severe penalties for false or misleading information
   C. Suing by investors through the courts for recovery of losses

3. The major exemptions from registration under the 1933 Act and the categories in which these exemptions fall are the following:

	Exempted Securities	Exempted Transactions
A. Private offerings to a limited number of persons who do not propose to resell		X
B. Intrastate offerings		X
C. Offerings of government or charitable institutions, banks, and common carriers	X	
D. Offerings of limited size		X
E. Offerings of small business investment companies	X	

4. Though not a requirement of the 1933 Act or the SEC, a comfort letter is a document to the underwriter and to legal counsel stating that nothing has come to the attention of the auditor that would indicate the registration statements are false or misleading.

5. By passing the 1934 Act, Congress attempted to:
   A. Regulate the trading of securities on secondary markets through brokers and exchanges
   B. Eliminate abuses in the trading of securities after their initial distribution

   Congress also realized the necessity to have an organization to carry out the function of the law. With the Securities Exchange Act of 1934, the SEC was established.

6. As measures to protect the investor, the SEC requires any investor who owns more than 10 percent of a registered company to
   A. File a report of holdings
   B. Report any changes in holdings
   C. Recover to the company or shareholder any gains on short-term transactions.

7. A proxy is a written authorization from a stockholder allowing another person to act or to vote on behalf of that stockholder at a stockholders' meeting. In effect, it is a power of attorney. With the broad base of ownership that exists in the United States, it is doubtful that a quorum could be assembled at the annual meeting of stockholders without the use of proxies. However, to make sure the stockholders are informed, companies must furnish a proxy statement containing considerable information in

connection with proxy solicitations. Regulation 14A is the SEC's comprehensive regulation for proxy solicitations for companies registered under Section 12 of the 1934 Act. Even if a 1934 Act company does not solicit proxies and therefore does not issue a proxy statement, it must supply substantially equivalent information to shareholders in an "information statement." The annual report to shareholders is basically the same as the required proxy material. Thus, proxy solicitation requirements provide a means of exercising broad disclosure powers for the SEC.

8. The purposes of the regulations covering a tender offer are:
   A. To prevent surprise "take-over bids"
   B. To allow time for the issuer to consider the tender offer

9. The Federal Reserve Board can regulate margins by raising or lowering them, and investment can be stimulated or curtailed this way. Thus, the margin problems that contributed to the 1929 crash can now be controlled.

10. The disclosure tools used under the Public Utility Holding Company Act of 1935 are registration and reporting—the same as under the 1934 Act.

11. The major purposes of the Investment Company Act of 1940 and the Investment Advisers Act of 1940 are control and regulation of brokers and dealers and investment companies.

12. While the provisions of the Foreign Corrupt Practices Act of 1977 are intended to deal with companies which have foreign subsidiaries or conduct business in foreign countries, they also deal with *all* companies which have securities registered pursuant to the Securities and Exchange Act of 1934. Thus, all public companies subject to 1934 Act requirements, whether or not they are engaged in foreign business or involved in corrupt practices, are also subject to the accounting, record keeping, and internal control provisions of the Foreign Corrupt Practices Act.

13. The Foreign Corrupt Practices Act of 1977 amends Section 13(b) of the 1934 Securities and Exchange Act to include the requirements for accurate and fair accounting records and adequate internal accounting controls. Accountants and other business people found not in compliance are now subject to severe civil and criminal penalties under the federal securities laws. It is also likely that accountants will feel pressure to expand their audit responsibilities in the direction of reporting on the adequacy of internal controls. While the total implications are not yet clear, it appears that the Foreign Corrupt Practices Act of 1977 will significantly affect the responsibilities and legal liability of accountants and others associated with U.S. business enterprises.

CHAPTER 3

1. The overall purpose of the SEC registration and review process is to determine compliance with the federal securities statutes. Those laws were enacted to offer protection to investors by providing full and fair disclosure of material facts concerning the sale of securities, and by prohibiting misrepresentation, deceit, and other fraudulent acts. The process is, therefore, designed to be preventive as well as corrective in nature. The purpose of the process is not to judge the merits of securities, nor does it guarantee accuracy of the information presented in registration statements and SEC reports. Investors are still responsible for their decisions, and managements and others associated with the statements are liable for the representations made.

2. Basically, the registration process for the 1933 Act includes:
   A. Selection of proper forms
   B. Request for a prefiling conference
   C. Submission of a registration statement
   D. Review by the SEC of the registration statement
   E. Preparation of the letter of comments
   F. Addition of amendments, if needed
   G. Acceptance of an effective registration

3. Since many statements are submitted for review, all members of the SEC's accounting staff are available to help advise registrants. Accountants should advise clients to take advantage of the available counsel; such action may help to save time and problems during the registration process.

4. The information required in the basic registration forms includes:
   A. The history and nature of the business
   B. The capital structure of the business
   C. The description of any material contracts
   D. The description of securities being registered
   E. The salaries and security holdings of major officers and directors
   F. The underwriting arrangements
   G. The estimate and use of net proceeds
   H. The financial statements

5. The normal examination of a registration statement by the SEC consists of a review of the statement and a comparison with other information available. Such a review is done by the Division of Corporation Finance. A branch chief gives a copy of the statement to an accountant, a lawyer, and an analyst. Memoranda are submitted by each of these three experts, and a letter of comments is drafted.

6. The letter of comments outlines the deficiencies that the review staff has found in the registration statement and makes comments as to how the document could be improved.

7. If a firm does not attempt to amend its original document, the SEC has three courses of action:

   A. It could let the statement become effective in a deficient manner, and the company would be liable.

   B. It could issue a refusal order. Notice must be given within 10 days of filing and a hearing must be held in 10 days concerning corrections.

   C. It could issue a stop order. This halts further consideration of the statement.

8. The Division of Corporation Finance can select from four different review procedures:

   A. A deferred review is evoked when the statement is so deficient that review is closed unless the registrant proceeds.

   B. A cursory review is a simple review which reveals no deficiencies and no comments are made. The advisers of the registrant provide letters of acknowledgement.

   C. A summary review is a limited review, nearly the same as a cursory review.

   D. A customary review is the longer, more involved review.

9. While waiting for its registration statement to be accepted and declared effective, the company can make an announcement of the prospective issue of securities.

10. In a preliminary prospectus, investment information must be disclosed but information as to the offering price, commission to dealers, and other matters related to price is contained in a final prospectus. The name "red herring" is derived from the words "preliminary prospectus" stamped in red ink on the front page. This informs the investor that the SEC review is proceeding and that the issue is subject to it.

11. Although not a selling document, a "tombstone ad" is an advertisement, such as those seen in the *Wall Street Journal*, to locate potential buyers.

12. To help prevent fraud by careful inquiry into the nature of the security being offered, the underwriters call a meeting of all involved professionals to discuss the issue. Final problems are resolved at this meeting.

13. The "pricing amendment" adds the actual offering price of the securities, the amount of underwriter discount or commission, and the net proceeds to the issuing company. This information is added to the front page of the prospectus (which is Part I of the registration statement). Little if anything

is changed from earlier amendments. The pricing amendment is usually the final amendment to the registration statement, which generally becomes effective within a few days through a request for acceleration of the effective date.

14. Among the major regulatory provisions a company is subject to under the 1934 Act are:
   A. Periodic reporting requirements
   B. Proxy solicitation requirements
   C. Insider trading requirements
   D. Tender offer requirements
   E. Accounting, record keeping, and internal control requirements
   (These are recent amendments under the 1977 Foreign Corrupt Practices Act and are not yet well defined.)

15. Pro forma financial statements included in SEC filings represent, for the most part, historical financial statements which have been retroactively restated, combined, or otherwise changed to give effect to proposed transactions, e.g., a pending merger or acquisition. Pro forma statements show the results of particular transactions "as if" they had occurred.

16. The 1933 and 1934 Acts are different in several respects:
   A. The 1933 Act regulates the initial offerings of securities; the 1934 Act regulates subsequent, secondary offerings of securities traded on stock exchanges.
   B. The 1933 Act requires a prospectus; the 1934 Act does not.
   C. The 1933 Act registers a specific security issue for a specific amount; the 1934 Act registers an entire class of securities which can be sold subsequently without additional registration.
   D. The 1933 Act does not have continuous reporting requirements; the 1934 Act does (e.g., the 8-K, 10-K, and 10-Q periodic reports).
   E. The 1934 Act is much broader in scope, requiring registration of companies, stock exchanges, brokers and dealers, and others.
   F. The 1934 Act contains provisions for very broad regulatory powers with respect to such areas as:
      1. Proxy solicitation requirements
      2. Insider trading requirements
      3. Margin requirements
      4. Accounting records and internal controls
   G. There are also some basic differences in legal liability under the two Acts.

17. In researching SEC accounting-related problems, the primary factors to be considered are the legal requirements of the statutes, as interpreted by SEC rules, regulations, and pronouncements; the reporting alternatives considered appropriate due to special circumstances; and generally accepted accounting practice, as supported by pronouncements of the FASB and AICPA. The disclosures presented should be logical and reasonable in light of the above factors, and there should be good documentation. The use of judgment is necessary because the answers are not always apparent from the statutes or SEC regulations.

The major sources of information to be consulted include:
A. The applicable Acts—the actual statutes containing the legal requirements
B. The instructions and guides to the forms, which provide information and the specific requirements for the various forms
C. The SEC Rules and Regulations, especially Regulation S-X and Regulation S-K. Regulation S-X specifies the general form and content requirements for the financial statements to be included; Regulation S-K specifies additional disclosure requirements, e.g., segment reporting information.
D. Other pronouncements of the SEC, especially the Accounting Series Releases (ASRs) and Staff Accounting Bulletins (SABs), which provide modifications and interpretations of reporting requirements and other actions of the SEC
E. The pronouncements of the FASB, AICPA, and other accounting bodies, which provide the basis for determining the generally accepted accounting principles that should be followed
F. See the Appendix for an annotated bibliography of selected references.

Chapter 4

1. Managements prepare two different annual reports, one for the SEC, the other for investors.

2. The significant changes in disclosure include:
A. The accounting profession and the SEC have recommended and encouraged increased disclosure.
B. Audited financial statements are required to be sent to investors.
C. Managements are cooperating better with the disclosure and reporting requirements.
D. Investors and especially financial analysts are demanding additional information about companies, e.g., segment data and forecasts.

3. Some of the more important disclosure requirements for annual reports are:
   A. Audited financial statements for the last two fiscal years
   B. A summary of earnings for the last five fiscal years and a management analysis thereof
   C. A brief description of the business
   D. A line-of-business or product-line report for the last five fiscal years
   E. Identification of directors and executive officers, with the principal occupation and employer of each
   F. Identification of the principal market in which the securities of the firm are traded
   G. Range of market prices and dividends for each quarter of the two most recent fiscal years
   H. A free copy of the 10-K report to stockholders upon their written requests

4. The most common forms sent to the SEC and the information contained on each are as follows:

Form	Information Contained
S-1	Information in prospectus Other additional financial items
Proxy Statement	Information to be given in connection with proxy solicitation
8-K	Notice of significant events impacting on the company
10-K	Annual financial reports
10-Q	Quarterly financial statements

5. The differences lie in the number of years for which a summary of earnings is required and the number of years for which certified financial statements are required.

6. Form 8-K must be filed with the SEC within 15 days after the end of a month in which a significant material event has transpired.

7. Extent of detail, number of years for which information is required, and certification requirements are among the differences in reports sent to shareholders and those sent to the SEC.

CHAPTER 5

1. The SEC has been granted broad statutory power
   A. To help it fulfill the goal of full and fair disclosure
   B. To help protect investors as a result of their dependence upon the opinion of experts such as accountants

2. The SEC gradually attained the broad power it now possesses. When the abuses in securities markets caused the market crash of 1929, some people felt accounting principles were to blame. The first Congressional grant was given to the Federal Trade Commission in the Securities Act of 1933. The FTC was given the power to prescribe rules and procedures it deemed necessary to fulfill its obligations under the law. In 1934 the Securities Exchange Commission was established and received additional authority over companies filing reports. Under the Public Utility Holding Company Act of 1935, the SEC can not only specify the regulations but can even prescribe accounting systems to be used.

3. Regulation S-X is a codification of the views and requirements in relation to the financial statements to be filed with the SEC. Regulation S-K is a set of integrated disclosure rules prescribing the requirements for nonfinancial statement data in SEC reports. Accountants dealing with SEC work should have current copies of both documents.

4. Accounting Series Releases primarily explain and clarify accounting procedures and practices needing special treatment in relation to disciplinary sanctions imposed by the SEC. Their purpose is to inform professionals of changing requirements and new SEC views. Staff accounting bulletins (SABs) are not official pronouncements of the SEC but represent interpretations and practices followed by the staff of the SEC in administering the securities laws. Thus, while not "official," they are important sources of information in working with the SEC.

5. Some of the instances where the SEC has exerted influence upon auditing standards and the significance of these influences are included below:

Item	Significance
McKesson and Robbins Case	Resulted in standards for observing inventories and confirming receivables
Yale Express Case	Resulted in standards for disclosure of subsequent events previously certified

Concept of Independence	Became part of the code of professional ethics; new disclosure requirements concerning nonaudit services incorporated in proxy statements
Fraud Detection	Resulted in accountants being used more extensively as policing agents
Auditing Procedures	Determined audit procedures

6. The accounting profession's view is that the audit is not intended to detect fraud. The SEC seems to be pushing auditors into the role of fraud detection. Accountants probably should accept more responsibility for fraud detection than they have traditionally.

7. The emphasis on legal liability can be attributed to several causes. First, managements and professionals have been subjected to damage suits stemming from their alleged negligence. Second, investors have been able to recoup their losses from the accountants or the managers who prepared and certified financial statements. And, more recently, an accountant's liability to third parties has been questioned. Then such precedent cases as *Ultramares Corporation, 1136 Tenants' Corporation, Continental Vending, and BarChris Construction Corporation* have focused more attention on legal liability. The *Hochfelder* case may limit the civil liability of accountants under Rule 10b-5. However, the extent of legal liability for accountants under the securities laws is by no means settled.

8. Current emphasis on accountants' legal liability concerns
   A. Liability to clients
   B. Liability to third parties
   C. Due professional care—ordinary v. gross negligence
   D. Awareness of current changes in auditing standards
   E. Liability under the Securities Acts

9. The essential objective of the SEC is to provide full and fair disclosure for investors. Therefore, the SEC has had a significant impact upon reporting requirements of businesses. The areas in which the SEC has evidenced influence include:
   A. Segment reporting by diversified companies
   B. Lease reporting
   C. Inflation accounting
   D. Reporting of "significant business uncertainties"
   E. Forecasts and forward-looking information
   F. Management disclosures, including remuneration and perquisites

10. The accounting profession has established an SEC Practice Section with specific requirements for membership. These requirements are aimed at improving the quality of accounting practice. One of the most significant aspects of the profession's program is "peer review," which involves the study of firms' quality control procedures. A Public Oversight Board has been established to monitor the progress of the accounting profession in its self-regulation efforts.

11. The Commission's philosophy has been to let the accounting profession develop and promulgate its own principles and standards and to establish additional requirements when deemed necessary.

12. The current trend of the SEC action in regard to accounting principles seems to be the tendency to take over where there are gaps or inadequate standards. Refer to current events.

13. This is an opinion question. Certainly there are arguments for both sides. However, the author would argue strongly for the private sector.